THE
PRACTITIONER'S
JOURNEY

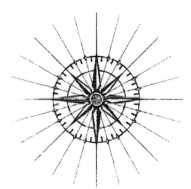

DAN CLEMENTS & TARA GIGNAC, ND

Library and Archives Canada Cataloguing in Publication

Clements, Dan, 1968-
    The practitioner's journey / Dan Clements, Tara Gignac.

ISBN 978-0-9739782-4-7

    1. Alternative medicine--Practice. 2. Customer relations.
I. Gignac, Tara, 1971- II. Title.

R733.C54 2010   615.5068   C2010-902217-3

TABLE OF CONTENTS

Introduction
The path to Success
-9-

Part I: The Cave
Solving the mystery of why practices fail
-17-

Part II: The River
Attracting new clients
-77-

Part III: The Boulder
Getting the most from your client base
-133-

Part IV: The Valley
Finding balance and building a sustainable career
-185-

Epilogue
The summit
-255-

Afterword
Love, life and legacy in health care
-259-

Never accept the idea that, because you are in business, you don't have the opportunity or time or personal qualities which a true spiritual life demands, or that maintaining a deep inner life is somehow contradictory with leading a business career.

The wisdom of The Diamond Cutter says that the very people who are attracted to business are exactly the same ones who have the inner strength to grasp and carry out the deeper practices of the spirit.

-Geshe Michael Roach
The Diamond Cutter

BEFORE YOU BEGIN

In this book we use a number of terms interchangeably. That's partly for convenience, but mainly because there's no generally accepted way of referring to the practitioners and consumers of the alternative health industry.

To describe the diverse industry we work in, we use the terms alternative, holistic, integrative, and complementary as they best suit the flow of the book, most often settling for "CAM" (Complementary and Alternative Medicine) as a catchphrase for all.

You might think of yourself as a therapist, a doctor, a healer, a practitioner, a coach or a counselor. You may own a practice, a business, or a clinic. You might work with clients, patients, or customers. Regardless of what language you use, this book will help you do what you do better.

In short, let's start by doing what great health care professionals have always done: forget about the labels and focus on what's inside instead.

And as for the people described in *The Practitioner's Journey?* They're all real. Just like you.

INTRODUCTION
The Path to Success

Many roads lead to the path, but basically there are only two: reason and practice.

-Bodhidharma

*I*f you're like most practitioners, your current practice is likely to take you to one of three places in the long run.

The first place is the scariest. It's called No Longer Practicing, and it comes as a result of just not being able to make it. After a few years of struggle, you still don't have enough clients to pay the bills *and* pay yourself, so you pack it in. It's a sad outcome, but sadder still is the fact that it's not that uncommon—in some CAM professions, it's rumored that as many as 50% of practitioners are no longer practicing within a few years.

The second place is called Getting By, and it's not nearly as scary, but it's not that great either. Practitioners in this category manage to find enough clients to get by, but they *just* get by. They feel like their practice sucks up all their cash, and they never really find financial freedom. They pay themselves when they can, but it's unpredictable. Cash on hand at the end of each month is usually zero, or a little less. Debt slowly creeps up. Enjoying work is a distant memory. Work and life are a constant struggle with little payback.

If that doesn't seem terribly enticing either, then consider the third possible destination: Burnout. It's a place of deception because on the surface it seems like a good spot to be. You have plenty of clients, a jam-packed schedule, and cash pouring in. The hidden dark side of this place, though, is the long hours, the deterioration of health and relationships, and, surprisingly, the continued financial struggle. After all, lots of cash doesn't necessarily mean lots of wealth, and many of these "super practitioners" are in just as much financial trouble as those who are Getting By. Burnout, it turns out, is simply a longer and more expensive route to No Longer Practicing.

There is good news, however. As of right now you're *not* like most practitioners. In discovering this book, you've just taken the first steps on a path toward an entirely different destination.

This destination is one that we've all heard of. It's called Success, but for all the legend surrounding it, few practitioners seem to find their way there. It's the Shangri-La of practice—a mysterious place where life is the way you imagined it before things got in the way.

Some pay a brief visit to Success on their way to Burnout, but they don't seem to be able to settle there for long. But we do hear the stories of those who have found their way, and those stories circulate through our professions in whispered tones at conferences, schools, and lunch dates. They are stories of a place where you find joy in your work. Where, in fact, you can't *wait* to get to work each day. Where you have the money you need. Where you work as much as you choose to work, but you love every minute of it. Success is the practice we dream of as students and covet as practitioners. It's a place where you help others find health and are healthy yourself.

The job of this book is to show you the way there.

TROUBLE ON THE PATH TO SUCCESS

By far the most extraordinary thing about Success is that so few practitioners actually find their way there. After all, a good look at our current state of health suggests that by all accounts, it should be a remarkable time to be in the healing professions.

Our aging population, deteriorating environment, and dangerous lifestyle habits are combining to create a tidal wave of chronic and acute illness the likes of which the world has never seen. To ride out the tide of this sickness tsunami, we're relying on an overloaded medical system that lacks the resources and philosophy necessary to cope. The result is a crisis of health, and a crisis of health *care*, that's driving people to seek alternatives.

Those alternatives are you and your colleagues: the chiropractors, acupuncturists, nutritionists, ayurvedic practitioners, massage therapists, naturopaths, and thousands of other holistic and alternative professionals out there. You're the life raft, and people should be climbing over each other to get on board.

Yet practitioners still struggle. On one side, we've got a market with a seemingly bottomless demand and desperate need. On the other, we've got practitioners barely getting by, or going out of business altogether. What's wrong?

After nearly a decade of running our health care business and teaching others to do the same thing, we've learned one critical thing: all practitioners face the same challenges. Whether you're a homeopath, a herbalist, a massage therapist, or a naturopath, the barriers to reaching Success are the same. Chiropractors, osteopaths, energy practitioners, and acupuncturists—they all face the same hurdles. **There are four challenges on the path to Success, and they're common to every holistic, alternative, or complementary practitioner.** Each challenge threatens to move practitioners off the path and send them wandering toward Burnout, Getting By, or No Longer Practicing.

This book is built around those four challenges. We'll get to them (and their solutions) in detail, but for now, here's a snapshot:

Challenge #1: Understanding the real reasons why practices fail

Why is it that some practitioners flourish and others fail? Why does one practice thrive while another disappears, even when they offer the same service? What is it about practices and practitioners that makes the difference between a trip to Success and a downward spiral to No Longer Practicing?

Challenge #2: Attracting a steady flow of new clients

A practice with no clients has no revenue source, and even an established practice that loses its supply of new clients will eventually shrink. How do you keep new clients arriving at your door, and how do you do it in a way that becomes less difficult and less expensive over time?

Challenge #3: Making the most of existing clients

Although new clients are critical, attracting them can be time consuming and expensive. It's very hard to reach Success without leveraging the clients you do have. How do you escape the constant treadmill of time and money spent seeking new clients?

Challenge #4: Building a balanced and sustainable future

Eventually, a busy practice leads to a busy life. And just as eventually, young practitioners become, well, less young. (Hey, it happens to everyone at some point.) How do you maintain your own health and energy as a practitioner while creating something of lasting value?

Those are the big four. Every book, video, course, conference, website, blog, and coaching program in the world of CAM practice development is about solving one or more of these challenges. It's that simple.

What's not so simple, as it turns out, is the way we *think* about solving them.

BEGINNING THE JOURNEY

For many of us, starting our practices is the day things become *complicated*. Confused by bills, leases, marketing, staff and other pressures of practice, we get caught up in worry, uncertainty, and fear. And once we reach that point, it doesn't take long for us to do what we do best when we're overwhelmed: shut down. And so we get up, we put one foot in front of the other for the day, and then we come home. Then we get up and do it all over again.

As a result, we keep pushing on without really pushing *ahead*. We go in circles, feeling like we're never quite making the progress we should for all our efforts.

The reason we find ourselves treading water like this isn't because the challenges of practice are too *hard*. It takes no special genetic or social advantage to reach Success. If you can attend school to learn to be a practitioner, then you're already blessed with all the advantage you need to succeed as one.

No, the hardest thing about the four challenges of practice is *thinking* about them in the right way. We have a habit of making these barriers too complex, too scary, or too overwhelming. And the more complex they become in our minds, the *less* we work to overcome them. We take one look at our to-do list and turn away just as quickly. We revisit the goals we carefully set six months before, and don't even know where to begin.

The more complicated we make the challenges of private practice, the further we drift from Success. **The challenge of practice, as it turns out, isn't solving complex problems. It's keeping things simple so that we can continue to move forward.**

Our job in this book is to simplify the four challenges that keep practitioners from becoming successful. *The Practitioner's Journey* is designed to take the thinking and actions that deliver success in private practice and distill them into a framework that you can easily grasp, easily remember, and easily put to work. Whether you don't know what to do, or you just don't know what to do *next*, this book will help you move toward the practice that fits you, your clients, and your life.

And your part? For now, that's the best part of all. You get to enjoy the ride.

For just a little while, forget what you think you know about this business of health care. Allow yourself to have what Zen Buddhists call *shoshin*, or "beginner's mind," and what we call "cutting yourself some slack." For just a few moments, shut down your internal critic and let yourself be willingly open to one phrase: *What If?*

What if your journey to Success as a practitioner doesn't start with trying to find new clients? *What if* it doesn't begin by developing a new marketing campaign or wondering if you should buy the latest technology? *What if* finding your way to Success isn't about how to choose the right office space or hire a new receptionist?

What if, instead of all those things, your journey to Success is much simpler?

What if getting from where you are now—whether it's the first day of school or the latest day of a long practice career—starts with something different?

Open your mind. Relax. And imagine that you're standing...

...at the edge of a forest.

Before you is a wide path that winds its way through the broad trees until it disappears from sight. The sun filters down through the leaves above, dappling the forest floor. All around you are the sounds of the woods. The gentle sway of the leaves rocking in the wind above. Animals rustling through the under-brush. The calls of birds echoing beneath the canopy.

To your right, a faded signpost points into the forest. Its paint is all but gone, the wood beneath weathered to a deep gray. You can faintly make out a single word carved into its weathered surface: *Success*.

Tacked to the signpost is a folded piece of paper. You look around, but there's no one in sight. Curious, you unfold it. It's worn, brittle, and yellowed by the elements, but still quite legible.

> *Fellow Practitioner,*
>
> *Welcome to the journey. The good news is that Success is not as far away as you may have been led to believe. To reach it, you need only what you carry with you right now. The rest you will find along the path.*
>
> *The rules are few and simple. To reach Success you need only do two things: follow the path to its end, and help as many people along the way as you can.*
>
> *Good luck and safe passage.*

With a last look around, you pocket the note and take your first steps on the path to Success.

✦

PART I: THE CAVE
Solving the Mystery of Why Practices Fail

One just principle from the depths of a cave is more powerful than an army.

-Jose Marti

As you enter the forest, you're relieved to discover that the path is wide and well marked. It's obvious that many people have come this way before, and you make good progress. In fact, the path is so easy to follow, and you're so excited about reaching Success, that you decide to keep walking after nightfall. *After all, you reason, the faster and longer I walk, the sooner I'll get there.*

The forest grows darker as the sun sinks in the west, but the path is still quite visible and you press on. Eventually you find yourself walking in complete darkness, moving ahead by watching the stars through the gaps in the trees overhead. The night is calm, the air warm.

You begin to think about what awaits you in Success. Days of energy and enthusiasm, nights of basking in the glow of a living earned by changing lives. It's a compelling vision, and it's some time before you become aware that *something has changed.*

Pausing to listen, you realize that the forest sounds around you have vanished. The rustle of leaves, the sounds of night frogs and insects—they've all disappeared. You look around and realize it's not just dark anymore—it's *really* dark. You can't make out any of the tree canopy overhead. There's no moonlight and not a single star.

You take a few tentative steps forward, but your footsteps have an echoing quality that wasn't there before. It's so dark now that you're afraid of blundering off the trail or hitting a tree, and so you hold your arms out in front of you and walk slowly forward.

Just as you're thinking this might be a good place to bed down for the night and wait until morning, your hands touch the rough, damp surface of a rock wall. It takes only a few more moments of fumbling about to realize what's happened.

The trail has led you into a cave and you're completely lost.

✦

Just a few short years after opening her Colorado practice in 2003, Tamara Hutchins had become a busy acupuncturist. "Through the first five years I had this amazing practice," she said, describing how her specialization in facial rejuvenation had paid off. "My practice exploded."

Prior to heading to acupuncture school, Tamara had spent several years as a massage therapist and she was now basking in the glow of yet another successful run. But in 2008, with the recession in full swing, Tamara's practice began to dry up, eventually dropping to just five clients per week. The run, it seemed, was over.

"I became so scared. I was dipping into my savings. Six months in, I couldn't take it anymore. I reacted. I put together my resume and went looking for sales jobs. It was terrible."

One day after a job fair, Tamara returned to her acupuncture office. Tired and discouraged, she sat down and looked around at the space she'd poured so much of her heart into. Sitting in her stiff interview suit she asked herself, *Am I really going to be selling photocopiers for the rest of my life?*

Tamara, like many practitioners, had found herself in the cave. It's the first obstacle on our figurative path to Success, and like the other challenges you'll discover in this book, the cave is a metaphor—a comparison we use to make things easier to understand and remember. Most of us never *actually* find ourselves trapped in a cave. But in our "real" world of clients and health care, the cave is as real an obstacle on the path to Success as any of the more tangible roadblocks of day-to-day practice like paying the bills and seeking new clients.

In ancient days, mapmakers often had limited information. Many of their maps had vast areas that were simply left blank because they *just didn't know enough*. The cave is similar. It's a blank spot on the map of our journey as practitioners. **The cave is a gap in our knowledge of ourselves, or our practices**, and, like the blank spots on the maps of ancient cartographers, that gap can have devastating consequences.

In fact, the cave is the single biggest reason that practices fail. While an ancient map might have labeled a blank spot with, "Here be dragons," our label might more accurately be, "Here's where things don't seem to be working and you don't have a clue why."

For some practitioners, the dark days of the cave begin early in practice when they first open their doors. For others, like Tamara, they appear without warning after many years of relatively easy progress. Regardless of the timing, though, the cave is the same for all: it's about being *lost*, figuratively speaking. And the problem with being lost in a cave in practice, just like in the real world, is that we can't make any forward progress. We're blind, isolated, and wandering aimlessly.

Most of what we perceive as "problems" in practice can be traced back to the cave. When the phone isn't ringing, when clients don't come back, when there's more month than there is money, we're experiencing *symptoms* of being trapped in the cave. When we agonize over why the practitioner down the street is busy when we're not, the real problem is that we're fumbling about trying to find our way back to the light of the path.

Why we become lost

The vast majority of CAM practitioners complete some kind of training before opening their doors. It might be a few weekend workshops, a few months of distance education, or a doctorate program lasting many years. Regardless of the length and style of that education, most training programs share one common problem: *they are considered to be enough.* When your training ended, it was assumed that you had the skills necessary to make your way in private practice. Sure, you might have continuing education obligations depending on your profession, but when school finished, you were *ready.*

At least, that's what we're taught. But in the real world of practice, **this assumption that students are ready to become practitioners as soon as they complete their health care training is at the root of almost every failed CAM practice.** It's like simply talking about what caves are like and then being sent deep inside one without a flashlight. Learn all you like and study all you want, but without a light, your PhD in Cave Studies is not going to get you out of the dark.

What *will* get you out of the dark days of private practice is an understanding of two critical principles that are the basic foundations for a vibrant future as a practitioner. Without them, it really is as if we're fumbling about in the dark, blindly groping our way to Success without any clue as to what direction we're headed.

The first principle you need in order to find a way out of the cave is about *you,* the practitioner—about the way you think, the beliefs you hold, and how they chart the course of your future. The second principle is about your practice—what it offers, to whom, and how.

Together they offer a way out of the dark days of practice and back onto the path to Success. To understand those principles, though, and how Tamara used them to rebuild her dying practice, we need to head back to the cave itself.

1. The Pool

The mirror reflects all objects without being sullied.

-Confucius

Once you realize your predicament—that you're lost in a pitch black cave—your first instinct is to turn around. You quickly discover, though, that all the fumbling about has left you thoroughly disoriented and you no longer know which direction is which. After accepting that you're completely lost, you stop walking (and stop bumping into things) and take a moment to consider what to do next.

The smartest thing to do seems to be to stay put until morning. With any luck, the sunlight will illuminate the entrance of the cave enough for you to find your way back out. But as you mentally debate spending a night alone in a cold cave, you notice that your eyes are starting to adjust to the darkness. The cave isn't as pitch black as you thought. You can make out faint outlines of stalactites hanging from the cave roof, and as you look around, you notice that the passage continues onward, toward what seems to be a faint glow.

Excited that you may have found a way out, you stand up and press on through the semi-darkness of the rough passage.

The light seems to increase with each step, and a few moments later you enter a rough rock chamber. At the center is a raised stone platform. As you watch, a drop of water ever so slowly drips from the end of a stalactite above and falls onto the platform with a gentle *plop*.

As the drop hits, you notice shadows ripple across the cave walls. You move closer to the center of the room, and you can see that the platform is actually a natural stone pool filled with crystal clear water. The stone around the water's edge casts a strange phosphorescent glow. Holding the edge, you lean forward for a closer look.

The combination of the water and the ambient glow turns the still surface of the pool into a shining mirror. You can see your own face reflected back at you in exact detail.

As you peer at your image, you feel rough grooves under your fingertips. You look down to find the following words chiseled into the lip of the stone pool:

PRACTICES REFLECT PRACTITIONERS

As you gaze into the still surface of the water, you ponder the message, and wonder how it can lead you back to the path.

✳

To unravel the first principle of the cave, let's leave the path for a moment and head back to something a little closer to home.

Imagine a busy street in your city or town. It's springtime and the warm morning sun shines on an unusual sight: two holistic clinics stand side by side, and through some unknown twist of fate, they are identical in every respect. They have the same office space. The same equipment. The same staff, the same paintings on the walls, the same carpet, and the same prices. In fact, everything about these two clinics, including their location, is identical. Each has the same startup cash and the same business hours. They even have the same *name*.

And today, both have the same signs in the window, which read: "Grand Opening."

Now imagine we drop two imaginary practitioners into the street, each with the same credentials. One heads to the clinic on the right, the other to its twin on the left. The door chimes ring in unison as they enter, and at the same moment both practitioners flip the signs on their matching front doors to "Open." Our two identical clinics are now in business.

Now fast-forward one year.

It's spring again and the morning sun shines once more on our two clinics. A steady stream of clients flows in and out of the first clinic's door, its chimes ringing pleasantly as each client passes. The other door's chimes, however, are quiet. The shades are drawn and it's hard to tell if the place is even open.

But it *is* open. The practices still have the same hours, the same equipment, and the same prices. But not *everything* has stayed the same.

If you could peek into the appointment books of the two clinics, you'd find evidence for what you already suspect. One clinic is busy, filled with clients seeking and receiving care. The other is practically empty, and struggling. If you could sneak a glimpse at their bank accounts, you'd find further proof. Another year like this one and the busy practice will need more space and more help. Another year like this one, though, and the quiet practice will be gone.

What happened? In a scenario where everything is equal, how has one practice fared so well and the other done so poorly? If we were to step inside each of the practices and try to identify the one thing that made the difference between struggle and success, what would it be?

That answer, of course, is that the single biggest determining factor for practice success isn't the practice at all. The greatest single factor that will determine whether or not your practice succeeds is what is reflected in the pool of the cave, and what you see in the mirror every morning: *the practitioner.*

Practices, as it turns out, don't fail or succeed. *But the people who run them do.* And if we confuse these two things, then we're making our first mistake in practice—a mistake that threatens to keep us trapped in the cave, unable to find our way back to the path.

Remember Tamara Hutchins? At the end of that fateful day of job hunting, she stood on the verge of abandoning everything she'd built. Despite her earlier experience and strong start, Tamara, like many practitioners, had entered the cave—that dark period in practice when things don't seem to work but we don't know *why*. What allowed Tamara to find her way out of the darkness, though, is what she did *next*.

"I sat down and had a moment with myself," she recalled. "I looked around at this space I had created, that I'd put so much love into. I thought, 'I'm a good acupuncturist. Why isn't this working?'"

That one simple question was enough to light the way forward. Tamara's insight in that moment was that *being a good acupuncturist wasn't enough*. She recognized that there was a gap in her knowledge—a blank spot in her map to Success. And unable to bear the thought of abandoning her sinking practice, Tamara resolved to find a solution.

Her first step was to contact Kevin Doherty, a practice management coach. From there she bought books on practice growth. "I absolutely believe that I became too comfortable," she said. She continued her business education, consulting with a business mentor who gave her further advice.

Her new knowledge in hand, Tamara began to shift her business from facial rejuvenation into more general practice. By 2009, things had begun to turn around. She was getting publicity on television and in print. A few months later, a little more than a year after hitting rock bottom at the end of 2008, Tamara's practice had become more successful than ever and she began looking at opportunities to expand into another city.

By 2010, Tamara had left the cave.

THE POOL: PRACTICES REFLECT PRACTITIONERS

What our identical practice scenario teaches us is that practices aren't the main engine of success. After all, if we can take identical *practices* and get different results, then success isn't really about the practice. It's about the *practitioner*.

So what really happened in Tamara's case? Like any practitioner who's found her way out of the cave, Tamara had discovered that it wasn't practical therapeutic skill that made the difference. Tamara, after all, is exceptional at what she does. She's highly trained, extremely personable, and gets great results. But her clinical excellence and bedside manner weren't leading her out of the cave or saving her sinking practice.

Tamara found her way back to the path by discovering the first principle of the cave: that *practices reflect practitioners*.

When she realized that being an excellent acupuncturist wasn't enough, she began filling the gaps in her knowledge, pursuing the business coaching, mentoring, and personal development she needed to become a practice *owner*, not just a practitioner. "It took me out of my clinical setting to realize, 'I need to put on the business cap and run this business.'" That effort was in turn reflected in her practice.

The pool is about continuing to develop yourself beyond the clinical skills you learned to treat clients. Tamara Hutchins found her way out of the cave not because she decided to take the reins of her business and increase her marketing, but because she realized that she had become complacent and hadn't learned *how* to do those things at the level she needed to in order to find success in a new economy. Her practice had become of reflection of her, and that reflection was no longer doing the job. The old Tamara—the one trapped in the cave—had created something that worked before. But as the landscape shifted, the old reflection of Tamara was no longer working.

In other words, Tamara didn't rebuild by working on her practice. She did it by working on *herself*.

Using the Message of The Pool

So how do you do what Tamara did? You don't need to hit rock bottom to find your way out of the cave, or to avoid it altogether. What's challenging, however, is that the message of the pool—the first insight of the cave—is difficult to "see." It's almost entirely invisible. It isn't tangible like your bank balance, your appointment book, or your office space. Yes, Tamara changed her marketing strategy, a tangible, observable action, but she began that change by first shifting her whole attitude towards how she approached her practice. Tamara changed her mind to change her practice, not the other way around.

It's an insight that runs contrary to the way most practitioners move through their careers. With a new diploma or degree in hand, the majority of us start working on our practices and stop working on *ourselves*. Other than the obligatory continuing education that our profession might demand, most practitioners, upon graduation, shift from personal development to practice development and never look back. From that time on, we spend untold hours working on our *practices*. We fixate on our physical office spaces, our equipment, our staff, and our clinical services. We spend thousands of dollars and a never-ending stream of energy working on the practice. What learning we *do* pursue usually involves a new clinical technique or other practical health training.

But of course that's understandable. Practices and the clinical care of clients are the most obvious and tangible parts of our success. What's more, they tend to be the squeaky wheel that attracts our time and energy. The space, the colors, the furniture, the signs, the staff, the computers, the equipment. Practices are so *physical* that they're difficult to ignore, and so we pour our time and money—and our hearts and souls—into them.

But to leave the cave, we need something beyond the physical practice—we need the message of the pool. Bodyworker Heather Furby from Santa Rosa summed up the pool perfectly when she told us, "A private practice is 100 percent personal development." To use the message of the pool, then, we need to do more than fill the holes in our practices. We need to fill the gaps in *ourselves*.

What are these gaps? Most of the blank spots on our maps aren't technical. The reflection of the pool isn't flawed by our lack of bookkeeping skills or the inability to create a website. The gaps in our maps run far deeper. The gaps are somewhere *before* the tactical steps we take to attract and treat clients. Remember that Tamara Hutchins made the decision to develop *herself* in order to develop her practice, not the other way around.

So where are the gaps? What's the difference between what Tamara did, and the simple actions of day-to-day business like more marketing? The difference is that before she could take action to change her practice, she had to change her *mind*.

For all its three pounds or so of mass, your brain holds a re-markably complex tangle of attitudes, ideas, opinions, facts, myths, and speculation. They're like shortcuts that help you navigate the world around you without having to pause for hours to decide what everything you encounter means. This framework helps us make faster decisions so we can get things done.

We call these frameworks *beliefs*, but you can call them what-ever sounds best to you. Just know that these paradigms—these ways of thinking about and interpreting the world—are determin-ing what you decide, and what actions you take. And those actions are, in turn, determining what your practice looks like and how it works out there in the real world.

Show the pool a practitioner filled with doubt about her skills, for example, and you'll get a practice that attracts doubtful clients—and not for long. Show the pool a belief that money is wrong, that health care should be free, or that business is some-one else's job and you'll get a practitioner who ignores the fact that he's paying more to run his business than he's earning. Over time (often a short time) that will be reflected by a practice that can't pay it's bills, and eventually goes out of business.

Your practice is a reflection of *you*. Your thoughts and beliefs are reflected in it. Your feelings about your practice, yourself, your clients, your modality, your finances, and your future—they're all manifested in how your practice operates, how much it charges, how busy it is, and the type of clients it attracts. If you believe that people don't like to pay for health care, then that belief will demonstrate itself in your practice. In fact, even if your *staff* believes it, then that belief will find a way to reveal itself in your practice. If you believe your job is simply that of a health care professional, then—guess what?—that will reveal itself in your practice, too.

Tamara's insight that she needed to put on her business hat in order to save her practice was a shift in her beliefs. Specifically, it was a shift in one of five false beliefs that keep us trapped in the cave. Deal with these, and you'll have no issues with the thinking and actions you need to move ahead on the path. They are:

1. Business is not your job as a practitioner
2. Money is unimportant or destructive in health care
3. Success happens quickly, or through enormous risks
4. You need a special aptitude or advantage to succeed
5. You can make any practice work

To align our beliefs with our journey to Success, we first need to understand three things about this tangle of attitudes.

First of all, most of these beliefs are subconscious. When asked about your position on money, business, or social class structure, you might find it challenging to articulate your beliefs. And yet they exist.

Second, these beliefs are learned. You weren't born with an attitude about wealth, work, lifestyle, money, or business. You acquired a way of thinking about these things over time and through innumerable experiences, big and small.

And third, since these beliefs were learned, they can also be *relearned*—that is, they can be modified, shifted, unlearned, or replaced with new beliefs that support your professional life.

FIVE NEW TRUTHS

Your first step toward finding success in your practice is to build a set of beliefs that are consistent, positive, and productive. A set of attitudes and ways of thinking that will support your path toward success in private practice, *however you choose to define it*. To make use of the first insight of the cave, there are five main truths that we need to embrace in order to master our "inner practitioner" and, as a result, create great practices.

Truth #1: You are in business

If you only take away one piece of advice from this book, make it this: as a CAM practitioner you have *two* jobs, not one.

Your first job, and the one you likely resonate with best, is that of healer/health care practitioner. It's what you studied to be. It's what you work at daily, and it may even be what you wanted to become from a young age.

The second job—the "hat" that might not feel comfortable just yet—is that of business owner. Most practitioners haven't given that role much thought. If you poll the ranks of the chiropractic, naturopathic, massage, and acupuncture schools, to name a few, you'll find a myriad of reasons why people attend, but few of them would be, "I wanted to start my own business."

You'll find a genuine interest in helping others. You'll hear tales of obsession with health and the human body. You'll even hear ambitious plans to reshape the future of health care or find a new way to bring health to even the most economically disadvantaged in all corners of the earth. But you won't hear many Trump-like tales of building empires. Most CAM practitioners enter their training with the goal of becoming healers, not business owners.

But there's a catch.

Most CAM professions remain largely unfunded by public health care systems. Coverage under private health care insurance plans lags far behind that of conventional medicine. Salaried positions are few. The vast majority of the revenue generated by CAM practitioners comes from private transactions with clients. If you're a CAM practitioner, then there's a good chance you're in business for yourself.

And there's the great irony of the CAM industry: **no one starts out to be in business, yet everyone has to be in order to succeed.**

It's not uncommon for practitioners to actively avoid this reality. Statements like "I just want to do my job" and "I'm here to help people, not run a business" are sentiments that we all feel at times. Unfortunately, they don't serve us as healers or as business owners, and they don't serve our profession.

If you're running your own practice, you don't get to choose whether or not to be in business—you already are. But whether or not you embrace your business and, like Tamara Hutchins, choose to become good at it is up to you.

If this is a bitter pill for you to swallow, then you need this book all the more. You can deny it, avoid it, ignore it, or pay it basic lip service, but to find success as a healer, you'll need to find success in business. The two are inseparable—the dualistic yin and yang of life as a CAM practitioner. But remember, *they are not at odds*. Even if your goals for your practice don't focus on money and wealth, *you're still in business.*

The good news is that this book is designed to help you understand that role and show you how to play your part to better serve your clients *and* yourself. For now, open your mind to the idea that inside you there really *is* a businessperson who can take on the role with grace, joy, and remarkable ability.

Truth #2: Money is an important part of practice

Profit gets a bad rap in health care.

To be fair, the quest for profit has done its share of damage. It's not without its problems. The horror stories of patients trapped by profit-driven health care systems have colored our collective consciousness.

The word *profit*, though, comes from the Latin word *profectus* meaning "progress" (or literally, to "make forward"). The use of the word to mean "making money" came hundreds of years later, and now few people remember the original meaning. And these days, despite its well-intentioned roots, the word *profit* (and by extension, *money)* is still a bad word in health care

For us, finding success in practice is closer to the old definition. It's about "making forward." It's about profiting in the original sense by continuing to grow, thrive, learn, and heal in all parts of your life—including the financial ones. In order to "make forward" in those other ways, though, you'll need to make forward financially, too.

That definition, though, is far from widely accepted. While the attitude that money is somehow inherently destructive, irrelevant, or unimportant can be found in any industry, it seems to run rampant in the CAM professions. Whether it's the natural predisposition of people interested in alternative medicine, or the training they receive, or some kind of cosmic force, CAM professionals seem to fall prey to this money-is-bad belief more so than other business owners.

Because most CAM professionals operate in a fee-for-service environment, any belief that doesn't support money as part of the equation has a way of showing up in practice. In fact, it's often the only thing that shows up—once the belief that money is negative appears, the money itself tends to stay far away. Perhaps Bowen therapist Amber Korobkina summed up this common sentiment best when she explained to us, "People who are controlled by money won't find success in the long run."

If this feels like you, then here are a few strategies for shifting your beliefs around money:

Think of money as a tool

Money is not wrong. Making money is not wrong. Money is just paper, or numbers on a screen. But it does one important job: it's a very effective tool that allows you to be a health care professional without people dropping off live chickens, hay bales, homespun cotton, and farm equipment as payment for your services. Money, to be more precise, is a convenient tool for measuring value and conducting business. If you thought being in business was distracting, try being paid for your services in cheese and fresh fruit. We've been there (really), and it's disruptive to say the least. Money is a convenient tool that makes being a practitioner a whole lot easier.

Think of money as an indicator of helping

In the world of CAM where insurance coverage is lacking, money can be a decent benchmark for *how much you're helping*. As

CAM tends to be a fee-for-service business, your clients are actively directing their disposable income towards your services—frequently with no option of recouping it from insurers. So if you're making money, it's because your clients are *choosing* to spend it on you.

The better you are, and the better your results, the more willing people will be to pay for your services. Give all your profits to charity if you choose (and without a doubt, giving back *is* an essential part of success), but know this: money might just be an indicator that *you're doing something right*. And that's nothing to be ashamed of.

Care about the money

A common sentiment among practitioners is that if they love what they're doing, then they shouldn't care about money. "People in our profession are phobic about saying they care about money," says Rolfer Brooke Thomas, "But they need to."

Pursuing your passion doesn't mean that you have to ignore the money. You may not want to do things that you dislike just for the money, but that doesn't mean you can't openly accept payment for doing the things you *do* love to do. Money is part of practice. Without cash flow you aren't able to pay your bills, and eventually that will mean you won't be able to practice, either. It's a reality, so acknowledge it.

That doesn't mean worship money, sacrifice your health for it, or give up your personal freedom or relationships for it. It doesn't mean you have to build a practice that only a lucky few can afford. It simply means that money is part of the equation, and to ignore it will eventually hurt both you and your clients.

The statistics for the CAM professions are frightening. Most practitioners struggle, and many don't make it. Acknowledging money is an important part of avoiding that fate. If you love what you're doing, getting paid appropriately for it gives you the freedom to do it more, and to do it in just the way you want to. It also allows you to do it better, and to sustain a longer career than you otherwise might if you were in constant lack.

Money, in other words, doesn't define Success, but it plays an important role in fueling the journey.

Own your fees

At some point after the marketing, the treatments, the phone calls, and the emails, there is a single activity that needs to occur: your clients need to pay for the products or services you provide.

How much do they need to pay? That's up to you to decide, but remember this: you must do more than choose your fees. You must *own* them. You have to have 100 percent confidence that your services are worth every penny that you charge. You need to be able to look any client in the eye, regardless of their income, and quote your fees.

Does it mean you need to set your fees high? No. You need to set your fees *correctly*, and that means matching them to the market and to what you offer. Your fees may not be the highest or the lowest, but they should most assuredly be *yours*.

How do you come to terms with your fees and, by extension, charge the appropriate amount? If you're like most practitioners, it can be enlightening (shocking, even) to add up *all* the expenses involved in running your practice for a month and then divide it by the number of client hours you have. And while you're at it, don't forget you're trying to earn a living—that means you can throw in all the costs of running the rest of your life—food, vehicles, accommodation, utilities, et cetera. And what about the costs to get you where you are? Student loans, business loans, and cash invested in education and startup. Of course, there's also the opportunity cost of those years spent in school—the many thousands of dollars you could have earned but instead missed out on while you trained. A monthly portion of that should be included, too.

Try it. You'll find that your time just might be a lot more valuable than you thought. Add up the cost of the eight years of post-secondary schooling required to be a DC or an ND, for example, plus the opportunity cost of not having a career during those years. It's hundreds of thousands of dollars. And that's just the cost of getting to graduation! Do the math and you'll realize that you've made a serious investment. So honor that investment when you choose your fees.

Part of owning your fees is coming to grips with the fact that you can't serve *everyone*. Feeling guilty for not offering free services is not helping your practice. If your business requires paying customers to survive, then someone who can't pay is a lousy customer. It doesn't mean they're a lousy *person*—don't confuse the two. To run a successful business you need to be able to define people in terms of their customer attributes without feeling like you're commenting on their value as human beings.

The fact that you're in the health care business doesn't mean you need to be a charity or offer ultra-cheap services. It's not that cheaper isn't a viable option (more on that later), but remember: although less expensive may mean more widely accessible, it still doesn't mean accessible to *everyone*. Boutique clinics with their higher prices exclude the less wealthy. Sliding scales and less expensive clinics exclude the profoundly poor who can't reach the bottom of the scale. Free clinics exclude the bed-ridden and agoraphobic. You'll always be excluding someone, somewhere—try to remember that you're *including* a whole bunch of others.

You can't help everyone. Building a successful business involves narrowing the world down to the slice that you *can*. Should you give back? Without a doubt. But it doesn't have to be in a way that destroys your ability to make a living.

In short, don't let your decision to run a good business make you feel like a bad person. If you want to give back, a failing practice isn't the best tool for the job. A strong business can be a powerful tool for good. Don't be afraid to discover that for yourself.

Truth #3: Success is the sum of many small steps

We live in a world of instant gratification. (In fact, that's likely why many of your clients end up in your office in the first place.) People want to buy it now, eat it now, and have instant wealth, instant health, and instant happiness.

Most CAM professionals have discovered that it can take time to heal a body. But our clients haven't figured that out yet, and so they enter our offices with chronic health conditions expecting immediate results. Most of the time a magic bullet simply isn't on the menu, and so we tell our clients to "give it time" or "stick with it." As educators and health care providers, we do our best to develop long-term relationships and lifelong views of health as a process, not a destination.

Ironically, though, after all that focusing on the long-term with our clients, we often head home and wonder why our practice isn't booked solid in our first month of business.

Physical health takes time, and so does business health. You might experience rapid "blockbuster" growth in your practice—and it's easy to want that—but remember, most things take time. Behind even the "blockbuster" growth stories are small actions executed over time.

There's a word for this approach to changing a business over time: *kaizen*. It's a Japanese word meaning "improvement," and it's come to describe a process of gradually getting better over time in business and in life.

Kaizen is a critical philosophy in *The Practitioner's Journey*. If you continue to believe that the journey to Success happens overnight, you'll continue to be overwhelmed by the huge changes to your practice you feel you have to make to get there. You'll continue to procrastinate from taking action in your practice, or continue to believe that it costs too much to reach Success. Until you believe that success is the cumulative result of small, steady progress, *you'll continue to believe that you can't do it.*

And that's a belief that just isn't true.

Truth #4: You have what it takes

Whether you're sitting in a classroom dreaming about your first days of practice or sitting in your office with those days far behind you, know this: you have what it takes to reach Success. **If you can help others, you can find your way to Success.** It's as simple as that.

Contrary to what you might think, *you can, in fact, make the journey*. You might be short on experience or information, but you're not short on talent. If you've made it to the point of being in practice, then you've already completed the hardest step of all. Practice success is not the sole purview of the movers and shakers, the business gurus, the driven, or the ultra-confident. If you've made it as far as working as a CAM practitioner, then you most certainly have what it takes to do it *successfully*.

It's normal to experience doubt. In fact, it's far more common than you think. None of us wants to admit to being doubtful, but we all feel it at times. Being told "don't worry" can be helpful, but it isn't always enough.

That's why working on yourself is so important. Continuing to learn and stretch yourself gives you perspective, knowledge confidence and companionship. When you attend a conference, for example, you may have second thoughts about spending the money. But then you return invigorated from the connection with colleagues and filled with new ideas for clients and practice, you've taken another step toward greater confidence.

Truth #5: Growth takes passion

Practitioner Andrea Ramirez's first career was as a musician. When she broke a finger in an accident, however, she was unable play for several months. But by the time her finger had healed, a part of her had changed: she realized that a life in music wasn't her calling. "I wasn't a musician enough," she told us. "If I had been, I would have done whatever it took."

Now, Andrea is a nutrition and lifestyle counselor for busy women. She's reinvented herself and started again in the holistic industry. But things feel different for Andrea this time. She has more passion. And that passion is what keeps her motivated through the dark spots.

"Building a business takes time. Not enough people talk about how long it takes to be an overnight success," Andrea said. And what keeps her going? Part of it is loving what she does and the people she works with. But another part of it is having a powerful *why*. Andrea currently lives in New York, but as she invests in her business, she imagines her goal of being location independent and one day opening her laptop in Barcelona, Spain to run her health care business that attracts clients from all over the world.

Passion like Andrea's is a critical ingredient. It's the juice of the journey, and we'd be lying if we said it's possible to reach Success without it. It's what'll keep you improving, changing, helping, and growing. We've all had the experience of being with someone who's incredibly passionate about what they're doing. It's contagious and inspiring, and when health care professionals have that same passion, their practices take off like wildfires.

You can't make *any* practice work. *Only the one that you're passionate about.* You've got to love the journey. If you're just in it for the destination, then obstacles like the cave become far more challenging than they should be. The destination just isn't enough. You need passion to fuel the trip.

HOW TO IMPROVE YOUR REFLECTION

It's one thing to read these beliefs, and another to make the shift towards internalizing them and turning them into real truths. Making that transition from knowledge to action is our next step.

How do you create a better reflection? One that, instead of being skewed like a funhouse mirror, is a clear, crisp image? It's one thing to say you need to learn to develop a positive relationship with money or to develop a financial IQ. But it's another thing altogether to actually *do* it. Here's how.

Dedicate regular time to personal learning and growth

Just like you might make marketing part of your regular activities for growing a practice, you need to make time for personal growth to learn about things like business, customer service, finance, psychology, and productivity. And when we say "make time," we mean carve it right out of your schedule, right now.

Schedule the time. If you need two days to take a seminar that's going to make a difference, then book it now.

Continuing to learn is the best way to develop the confidence and awareness required to change the way you see yourself and your practice. Make the time for it.

Invest in yourself

In addition to time, you'll have to spend money, too. Not necessarily a lot, but at least some. And you'll need to adjust to the concept of investing real money in *yourself*.

This isn't new to most practitioners. We all paid something to get where we are. But after our investment in our training, many of us don't continue to invest in ourselves beyond the minimal continuing education work that our professions might demand. And it's even more rare for us to invest in non-health care related personal development. As Andrea Ramirez told us, "You have to invest. The challenge is that in practice, much of the investment is invisible. If you invest in a restaurant, you can see that investment. When you invest in yourself, it's not as visible. I've had to invest in learning how to make money."

Don't be afraid to buy books, get coaching, take seminars, or listen to audio programs. They are truly valid investments and will pay off many times over. For most practitioners, it only takes a handful of client visits to recoup an investment. A single insight gained from a business course, for example, can deliver thousands of new dollars every year.

And yes, you can learn a lot for free. But there are times when you can make huge leaps only by making a financial investment in yourself. Money doesn't necessarily equate with value, but there's something special about doing more than just reading a free library book or searching the internet. Sometimes making a financial investment creates *perceived* value—it makes us feel that the thing we've invested in is *worth* more. That can lend a sense of increased accountability and push us to make the leap from simply learning something to actually putting it to use. One practitioner we met with spent tens of thousands of dollars on a yearlong coaching program to help her grow her business. It was a big investment in knowledge that she could likely have found elsewhere for a fraction of the cost. That big investment, however, lit a big motivational fire. She got her money back many, many times over—in part because her initial investment was large enough that she put serious effort into the program.

How much should you invest? Personal development blogger Steve Pavlina recommends investing three percent of your income in your own development.[1] You can choose your own level, but to master your inner practitioner you need to make the same commitment to *personal* development that you would to maintaining your license or paying your rent.

Treat inner growth as part of your job

One of the toughest things for practitioners to see is that personal growth is a necessary and useful part of practice success. When we're writing checks, seeing clients, or marketing, we feel as if we're making valuable contributions to practice success; we feel we're being *productive*. But reading a book about personal development? It feels like we're not really *doing* anything.

Don't believe it. If Tamara Hutchins had believed it, she'd be selling photocopiers instead of practicing acupuncture. Her decision to take the reins of her business by developing herself as a practitioner saved her practice, and if you were to ask Tamara, she'd likely say that it saved her, too.

Many professions require that practitioners participate in continuing education to maintain their licensing. And because it's a requirement, most practitioners get their CE credits through various types of ongoing learning sources like books, courses, conferences, and traditional schooling. Your personal development should be the same: a *requirement* that you meet in order to find your way to Success.

Remember that in the long run, working smarter is going to get you further than working harder. Both are essential ingredients, but the hard work needs to be directed by the smart thinking that only comes from making personal growth a priority.

Don't lie to yourself

In our figurative cave, the pool reflects your true self. In the real world, though, the mirror in the bathroom doesn't work the same way. It's far too easy to lie to that one. If you want to improve your reflection, you need to do it by being continually honest with yourself.

If you're not happy in practice, *admit it*. It's a sign that your passion is lacking. It doesn't mean that you need to stop practicing, but it's an indication that something's wrong. Finding it and fixing it starts with admitting it.

If your business is doing poorly, admit it. Don't pretend that you're doing okay financially if your credit card payments and other debts are climbing every month. If you're having trouble keeping clients, acknowledge it. It's likely something you can fix (more on that later), but fixing it starts with being honest about it. You can't get to Success until you truly see that image in the cave for what it is and resolve to improve it.

Imagine the future

Right now it might feel like your practice is just right (although, if you're reading this, that's likely not entirely true). It might seem that you really don't need to embrace growth, or transition from practice to business, or get involved in any of the stuff that this book covers during the journey to Success.

But cast your thoughts forward. Imagine a time when you've been in practice for twice as long as you have been now. Then imagine a time when you're twice as old, or when you might have children (if you don't already), or when your children have left home. These are different stages of life, and with them come different ways of thinking. Although it's hard to believe now, you may feel differently one day about your practice. You may have different priorities.

Thinking forward changes the way you perceive *now*. Don't limit your future practice and lifestyle by the way you feel about your practice *today*. Keep your future options open by embracing the idea that you will change over the course of your career. A practitioner who is open to change is a practitioner who can shift her reflection when challenges arise.

How important is the reflection in the pool? If you're tempted to disregard this as fluff, think again. Practice success is *all* about your mindset and how you choose to think. The work-life balance and financial success that you discover in your practice will be entirely built on the manner in which you choose to develop your inner practitioner.

If you're still skeptical, consider this: Dunn and Bradstreet, the company that's been tracking business financial health since 1841, reports that of the businesses that fail, 90% do so *because of a lack of skills and knowledge on the part of the business owner*. Other experts report similar reasons. When the dust settles, it's not competition, the economy, lease rates or government regulations that make or break businesses. It's what's inside the business *owner*.

The tools you use, the products you choose, the people you hire, the rules you make (and the ones you break)—all of those things appear first in your mind. There's nothing mysterious about this process. It's not complex. It's a simple formula that's applied day-by-day, for as many days as there are, and the formula is at work whether we want it to be or not.

Practices reflect practitioners. Call it magic. Call it logic. Call it what you like. You can look at it through the lens of metaphysics and attraction, or you can see it as psychology or physics. Call it neurology or call it karma, or just think of it as the practical outcome of applied focus. Think of it however best fits your worldview, but *accept it.*

Your inner practitioner—what the pool is reflecting—is fundamental. The steps that follow in this book are all built on that foundation of a strong inner practitioner.

But does this mean that your practice doesn't matter? Of course not. Working on yourself may be the most fundamentally important part of practice success, but it's not the only part.

There's more to that blank spot on the map than just developing yourself. After all, staring at your reflection in the pool isn't going to get you out of the cave.

To do that, you'll need something else.

2. The Crystal

If you do things well, do them better. Be daring, be first,
be different, be just.

-Anita Roddick, Founder of The Body Shop

fter some time in the cave, you find yourself
once again exploring the stone chamber, but
returning over and over to the glowing pool at its
center.

As you gaze at the still surface of the pool, another drop falls
from the ceiling above you, spreading ripples across the water's
surface, disrupting the perfect reflection. As the ripples spread,
you notice that you can now see *into* the pool. There is something
resting on the stony bottom.

You reach into the water and lift to the surface a glistening
crystal, its sides so clear that it was barely visible when submerged.
Turning it over in your hands, you can make out a faint inscrip-
tion on the bottom:

DIFFERENCES ATTRACT

Curious, you sit back against the stone pool and ponder the
strange gem. As you turn it in your hands, though, you realize
that the pool itself has grown dark. The glow in the chamber is
now coming from the *crystal.* You hold it higher and it casts a dim
glow that gently illuminates the rough walls of the cave.

Breathless, you scramble to your feet. Holding the crystal in
front of you, you're able to see just well enough to make your way

around the chamber. And after a few minutes of searching, you find another tunnel branching off. With relief you follow it, and within minutes you can see the glow of daylight ahead.

Moments later, you're standing at the mouth of the cave, squinting into the bright morning sunlight. The path stretches ahead, just as it did before you entered the cavern the night before. Relief washes over you.

As you walk the path, your mind calms and you think back to the second message of the cave—the one inscribed on the crystal. What does it mean?

You pull the crystal from your pocket for a closer look, but as you bring it into the sunlight it seems to change before your eyes. In the cave the crystal had a soft guiding glow, but here in the light of day it's as if the gem has been supercharged, magnifying the sun's rays and projecting them in every direction. Even in broad daylight the light arcs across the sky, visible for miles around.

Watching the beams of light disappear from view behind the trees, it hits you. The crystal that guided you through the dark has another purpose, too: it's a beacon for others.

When Maya opened her chiropractic practice in the 1990s, it didn't take much to get started. There were already a handful of DCs in her part of the city, but the market was by no means saturated. With little fanfare, she set up shop in the office of another practitioner and hung out her shingle.

Maya was a great chiropractor with an excellent technique and strong bedside manner. Her practice grew quickly and referrals skyrocketed, boosted in part by the busy practitioner who had first taken her on. Life was good and practicing was easy.

At least, that's how it was for a while.

Things changed, like they always do. Over the next decade, more and more DCs moved to the area and her profession took several painful blows in the public eye. Today, her neighborhood is overflowing with chiropractors just like her. Nearly everyone has less business than they'd like, and more chiropractors are arriving each year. The latest one, in fact, opened her office just a few doors down from Maya's clinic. Both Maya and her practice are being slowly drained of clients, cash, and enthusiasm.

Contrast Maya's experience with that of Andy Rosenfarb, an acupuncturist and naturopath in New Jersey. Andy sees 200 to 250 clients per week. Not only is he attracting them locally, but they're also *flying in from all over the world* to see him. The difference? The difference is just that: Andy is *different*.

What makes someone fly halfway around the world to see an acupuncturist in New Jersey? In Andy's case, 70 percent of his clients are consulting with him because of vision issues. Andy's an expert in using acupuncture and herbal medicine to treat vision-related conditions like macular degeneration, glaucoma, and diabetic retinopathy. He's created a worldwide market by carefully carving out a niche for himself in what might have been a crowded area. Where Maya's practice is slowly bleeding out in a jam-packed market, Andy's is thriving in one that's almost boundless.

Andy, in other words, has found his crystal.

The crystal is about defining your difference. It's about finding that thing that makes your practice unique in its own way. In our story, it's the bright light that serves as a beacon to attract others. In practice, it's your own unique "shine" that attracts clients to you when they might otherwise stay home, see another similar practitioner, or stick with conventional care.

Remember those two identical practices? The ones with the same signs, the same prices, the same location—even the same *name*? The purpose of that unlikely scenario was to demonstrate the importance of the practitioner. But what about the *practice*? Is the idea of identical practices really so far-fetched?

Pick up a business directory and look under alternative medicine, or pick a specific profession like massage therapy or naturopathy. You'll find more green leaves, yin yang symbols, and serene-looking women than you can shake a stick at. You'll read names like "The Wellness Center," "The Holistic Health and Wellness Center," or "The Holistic Family Healing Clinic." If we asked you to distinguish between them five minutes later, you probably wouldn't be able to recall which was which. Search online and you'll find more of the same... *sameness.* Walk the street and you'll see similar-looking clinics offering similar services at similar prices in similar ways to similar people in similar rooms across the country. You don't have to look far to realize that the idea of identical clinics really *isn't* that far-fetched. It's happening all around us, and it's a practice killer.

If you head off down the path to Success looking the same as everyone else, it's going to be a very long journey. While the pool is about making the most of what's in *you* so that your practice can reflect it back, the crystal has a different message. It's about your *practice*—about how to set it apart from the other things that fight for the attention and resources of clients.

Why you need to be different

In the real world, the crystal has many different names. Some call it a "unique selling proposition," others a "niche," and still others a "value proposition." We just call it "being different in a way that matters" because that's easier to understand. Regardless of the label, finding your difference is critical to success.

Your difference serves two fundamental purposes: to guide your decision making and to attract others to you. Or, to stick with our metaphor, to help find your way through the darkness of the cave and to attract new clients in the light of day.

The challenge for Maya and her colleagues was more than just simple competition and shifts in the industry. After all, there are many crowded industries with plenty of competing businesses, yet those industries all have their own shining stars—companies that thrive in spite of competition. Many, in fact, who thrive *because* of it. In the case of Maya's city, there were no shining stars and everyone suffered.

The problem for Maya was that her practice was no different from anyone else's. Beyond the fact that she was very nice and very good at what she did, prospective clients had no reason to choose one chiropractor over another—in her industry, *nice* just wasn't enough. Even the loyal client base that Maya had developed through the years couldn't sustain her forever. Their referrals were diluted by too many choices. Why pick Maya when there was someone else closer, cheaper, or open later? For every client referred to Maya who arrived at her door, two others might pick another clinic simply because *it didn't matter.*

In short, Maya was a talented, personable practitioner. *She was special.* But her practice—what she offered, to whom, and how—was *not.*

Simply offering "chiropractic" or "acupuncture" or "massage" or "holistic nutrition" is not enough to build and sustain success in the long run. You need to discover your difference, your beacon that can attract and hold clients. You need to find your crystal.

If you're not convinced, here are a few compelling rewards for defining your difference:

Stand out from the crowd

Just like our chiropractor Maya, there needs to be a difference between you and your competition. Those people thinking about seeing a massage therapist for the first time? They need a reason to choose *you* over the practitioner down the street.

Withstand future competition

Don't have any competition, you say? You will at some point. If you've already built a great client base, then your difference will help you hold onto it when competition comes to town. When there's little or no difference between you and another practitioner, customers can switch to someone else closer, cheaper, more convenient, or faster anytime they like. It's up to you to give them a reason not to.

Stand out from "nothing"

The biggest source of new clients for your practice isn't the people who already use your particular brand of medicine. At the moment, most people *don't* use your modality. They're at home right now busy *not* being your customer. So what is it that's so special about your offering that will make them want to go from being non-customers to being devoted CAM users? Or to expand beyond the conventional care they're currently using?

Make sure new referrals arrive

Unless you're different, referrals to you can inadvertently become referrals to your competition. What's the difference between "The Wellness Clinic," "The Holistic Clinic," and "The Natural Health Clinic" in the eyes of a new client? Sure, it's obvious to *you*, but you're not the newbie who needs to choose the right clinic from a list of possibilities. When your raving fans refer people to your clinic, is your clinic distinctive enough to ensure that they arrive?

Make sure referrals are to you, not to your modality

Let's say you've got a fantastic, perfect client who loves your services. We'll call him Colin. He sings your praises from the rooftops, extolling your virtues to anyone who'll listen.

Or does he? Is Colin telling people that they need to visit *your* homeopathic clinic, or is he simply telling people that they must try *homeopathy?* If you haven't educated Colin as to your difference (or if you just don't have one), who's to say that Colin is even referring people to you to begin with? He may think he is, but the reality might be quite different.

Make marketing easier

After struggling to make her business work, nutritionist Stacey Weckstein took some time off to refocus. "There was this disconnect between my personal life and my professional life," Stacey recalled. "Who I was as a person didn't fit with who I was in my work."

With some help from Karin Witzig Rozell, founder of Well-ProNet.org, Stacey found a target market that fit her: business owners. For Stacey, they represented a group of people who wanted to take action and get results. She refocused her message and marketing materials, and reopened her Florida office.

The result was a more confident, focused practice and practitioner. "I'm much more self-assured when I talk to people," Stacey says. And the job of promoting her practice has become far simpler. "Now when I write a newsletter, I have a specific person in mind. When I speak with people, I'm not trying to sell, I'm trying to find a fit."

Make easier, better decisions

Understanding your difference makes it easier to decide where to advertise, when and how to hire staff, when to buy new equipment, and what services to offer. Because your difference helps you define who you offer your services to, that difference also gives you a reference point for what's worthwhile to spend money on and what isn't.

Build a business that's worth something

We place a lot of emphasis on building something of value in this book. Being different means that your practice is worth more. The defining difference that makes you stand out in the marketplace also makes your business worth more to someone else in the future. Why would someone pay top dollar for your practice if clients can readily jump ship to another?

DIFFERENT KINDS OF DIFFERENCE

If you're cringing at the thought of trying to find a specialty, fear not: you don't *have* to. Picking one condition or illness isn't a requirement for success. Specializing is just *one* way to be different.

Similarly, being different doesn't mean you have to offer a unique type of health care that no one else in your market is offering (although, as we'll see, that is one way to be different). It doesn't mean being weird, or way "out there," or controversial, or bleeding edge (although they can work, too).

Here are several ways to differentiate your practice in the busy world of CAM treatment. Each is like a facet on the crystal, or the cut, clarity, and carat of a diamond. They're unique aspects of your practice that make you distinct from those around you.

Facet #1: Specialization

Andy Rosenfarb's vision-based practice is specialization at work. It's focusing on solving a *specific health problem*.

"In my opinion," he told us, "specializing is the single best thing you can do for your practice. The public is used to going to see conventional doctors who specialize and have become comfortable with this model of health care." For Andy, specialization is an insurance policy for his practice. It's guaranteeing him a market and a steady flow of clients.

Andy's right about conventional care. For many years, the medical profession *has* been an example of increasing specialization. The role of the GP has commonly become one of referring to professionals skilled in a particular area. Doctors are finding a market (and increasing wealth) as pediatric oncologists, neurosurgeons, cardiologists, and obstetricians. And the specialization continues. Family doctors become surgeons. The surgeons become cosmetic surgeons. The cosmetic surgeons specialize again, focusing solely on breast augmentation.

Why do they do it? After all, it can take years of additional work to develop the highly specialized skills necessary for these areas. Why bother? It may seem that doctors do it for wealth (partly true) or prestige (also true), but another reason why these doctors specialize is to be *different*. It ensures that referrals for eye surgery come to *them*. It helps sway prospective clients from another clinic to theirs, and deliver all of the other benefits that we mentioned at the start of this chapter.

The same approach can work for your holistic practice, too. When Aranka Jones opened her doors as a new naturopathic doctor, she was doing so within a few blocks of several other naturopaths in a small community. Her difference? She specialized in cosmetic naturopathy. Her business, Sakura Naturopathic Medical Spa, is based on Aranka's passion for providing women with non-toxic alternatives to conventional beauty products and to use naturopathy to enhance beauty from the inside out. Her belief is that the women in her target market are often willing to invest more in their hair and makeup than their health. By offering beauty side-by-side with naturopathy, she's able to attract new clients that might never have considered her services otherwise.

Is specialization always the right solution? That depends on what you offer, and to whom. For Andy and Aranka, choosing a specialty has made a huge difference. In the case of acupuncturist Tamara Hutchins, though, she needed to do the opposite and expand into more general practice in order to grow enough to make her anti-aging specialty sustainable. How can you decide? Here are a few factors to consider:

- How big is the population you're drawing from? It might be hard to specialize in a small rural town of only a few thousand people.
- How much competition do you have? Like Aranka, specializing might be the way to shine in a crowded market.
- Is your treatment modality well understood? Many CAM therapies aren't well known. A specialty can help attract people who might not consider you otherwise. While few people might know of Bowen therapy, they'll clearly understand the idea of someone who specializes in chronic pain.
- Are you geographically specific? If you offer some services online or by phone, for example, then you have a worldwide market to work with. Specializing can make it easier for you to find clients in a busy online world.
- Do you have a passion? Aranka wants to detoxify and "green" her community, one bathroom vanity at a time, and encourage women to pursue beauty from the inside out. It's something that she's passionate about, and it

shows in her practice. If you're that passionate, why do anything else?

There's nothing stopping you from having more than one specialty, although each requires a level of knowledge, effort, and focus. What's important is that specializing can be an effective way to find your crystal.

Facet #2: Market Niche

While Andy and Aranka may have focused on a specific issue or condition, choosing a *niche* is slightly different. A market niche is a specific group of *people*, not problems. Nutritionist Stacey Weckstein, for example, focuses on one group of people (business owners) who have a host of *different* problems.

When chiropractor Steve Rallis turned his focus to the niche of corporate wellness, the results were almost instantaneous. Steve had developed a unique health risk assessment technology called HealthScore. Though it's now used by scores of practitioners in different fields, it was the niche approach that gave Steve his first foothold in the market.

"My first corporate client earned me more that month than my entire private practice," said Steve. "It felt like overnight success."

You can focus on athletes, women, children, blue-collar workers, artists or any one of a multitude of groups of people. The choice is yours. Like specialization, however, choosing a niche requires that you ask yourself the same questions (see previous page) to make sure your choice is right for you and your market.

Niches and specialties tend to go hand in hand. Choosing a *niche* like women, for example, often leads to a *specialty* in areas such as menopause or fertility.

Facet #3: Being the best

Closely related to specialties and niches is the idea of simply being number one. It's hard to compete with the best, particularly in health care. People may not care about buying their car from the best dealership in town, but they *love* to see the best doctor. It's one reason why specialists get business: their narrow field of practice makes them really good at it.

There are a few challenges to being the best, though. The most obvious is that you actually need to *be* the best, and by definition, there can only be one best. Fortunately, there can be a best for each niche, and best tends to be a subjective term. The reality is that there are often several "bests" in a given field.

It is, however, difficult to be the best when you're just starting out. Being the best requires an investment of time and there are very few shortcuts, but there's nothing stopping you from getting started. Everyone who's an expert now started somewhere.

Facet #4: Price

One of the most common strategies for being different is the price of your offering. More specifically, it's usually having the *cheapest* price that offers an easy way to stand out from the crowd (although being the most expensive has a strange allure all its own).

This strategy is most commonly applied to commodities—mass-produced goods that aren't that different from one another and that have no other way to compete. When was the last time you were really particular about your brand of gasoline, for example? All things being equal, you likely just buy the cheapest.

But while this strategy is great for products, it's a bit tougher to apply it to health care. The challenge with being the cheapest is that you still need to make a profit to stay in business, and selling your services cheaply makes that more difficult—particularly in health care, where the costs of training, facilities, equipment, and supplies tend to be high. In the service industry, there will always be someone who can come along and offer his time for less than you can offer yours. And in places where health care is publicly funded, the lowest price is *free*. That makes competing on price even more challenging.

It turns out, however, that you *can* create a difference based on price and still make a living. It really can be done—we'll look at how later on. For now, let's assume that price is indeed a power-ful difference, and the future of CAM does not rest solely in the hands of "boutique" (high-priced) practices.

Facet #5: A unique offering

In a way, all of these forms of differentiation are about creat-ing a unique offering. In this case, though, what we mean by "unique offering" is a product or service that no one else has.

Are you the only practitioner certified to offer a certain treatment? Is yours the only clinic in town with a specific assess-ment tool? Being the only source of a product or service provides you with an instant advantage. Is the experience at your clinic a unique one that no one else can provide? Do you have a unique setting? Your own protocols?

Consider chiropractor Mike H. When he brought the first spinal decompression machine to his area, his client base ex-panded simply by virtue of the fact that he was the only one who had the technology. Investing in the equipment and training opened up two new key markets for Mike. The first was those people who had never considered chiropractic adjustment. They sought him out for non-surgical spinal decompression, and over time many came to embrace a broader chiropractic philosophy as well. The second new market was clients of other chiropractors who began to switch to him because he was the only chiropractor in the city to offer the new treatment.

For Mike, being the first and only practitioner with a new technology created a huge difference.

Compare Mike with another chiropractor we know of who does house calls *only*. He has no office space and very little overhead. He drives to clients' homes with a portable table. That's his difference. It appeals to a very specific group, which he's pleased to cater to at a premium price. What's more, his costs are little more than phone, banking, and transportation. Both these professionals are chiropractors, but each has a unique offering—a crystal that gives him an edge in attracting and keeping clients.

Facet #6: Service

Since CAM is, by its nature, largely service-based, why not provide *excellent* service? Go the extra mile for your clients and they'll make note of it. Word will get around.

Providing excellent service in your practice, though, takes more than just effectively treating health complaints. "Customer service" is really another term for the customer *experience*, and that experience reaches further than most people realize. Our tendency as practitioners is to focus more narrowly—perhaps just on the client visit—but the *complete* customer experience is much more expansive. It covers everything from how easy it is to find your website to how much parking is available, from how quickly phone calls are returned to how easy it is to pay.

The good news is that it's not necessarily expensive to provide exceptional service. Much of what makes a client experience a great one can be achieved with very little cost. Most great customer service isn't committing to a big budget; it's simply being dedicated to the *idea*. It doesn't cost more to care, to be respectful, or to be thoughtful and kind. But it does require a commitment to thinking of your clients first—and surrounding yourself with people who will do the same.

In our clinic, for example, the new year often starts with numerous requests from clients for summary reports of their invoices over the past year. Many need them for tax or insurance purposes. It's not a big deal, but in the middle of a busy day it's one more thing for the staff to juggle while the phone's ringing.

We could charge for that service and make a few bucks, justifying it by saying that it takes time and paper and ink to generate the reports. But is that good service? When the question of summary reports first arose, we looked at it through the filter of our philosophy of excellent service. We imagined that we were the client, who has spent perhaps thousands of dollars that year at our clinic, and all she asks in return is for a piece of computer-generated paper. How can we charge for that? Anyone who's visited our clinic enough times to need a summary report of her year's activity should be given a *gift*, not another invoice. So instead of charging for what is a bit of a distraction and an annoyance, we offer it with a smile and a great big "thank you."

For our clinic, where the client experience is a critical part of our difference, making the extra few dollars would be far more costly in its crippling effect on the client experience. People constantly return (and refer) to us because we bend over backwards to serve them in a way they don't experience elsewhere.

Facet #7: Access

Closely related to customer service is the perception of how *accessible* you are. Are you open 24 hours a day? Evenings? Are you the closest? Do you have the most easily accessible clinic with the best parking? Can new clients always get a same-day appointment? Do you offer house calls? None of these may appeal to you, but each is an opportunity for differentiation in a crowded marketplace.

Facet #8: Philosophy

One of the great opportunities presented to you as a CAM practitioner is to define at least part of your difference through your health care philosophy.

As conventional medicine continues to struggle with the declining health of an aging population, and as the pharmaceutical approach to health care comes under increasing scrutiny, the CAM professions become differentiated simply by the fact that they are, indeed, *different* from conventional care. The term "alternative" suggests a difference simply by definition.

Remember, though, that your difference isn't just the fact that you offer herbal medicine, homeopathy, or chiropractic. Those tools need to be backed by a philosophy that will resonate with potential clients.

CRYSTAL MINING: FINDING YOUR DIFFERENCE

There are as many ways to be different as there are practices, and many have yet to be discovered. Companies like Cirque du Soleil and The Body Shop arrived in established or dying industries and succeeded beyond any wildest dreams simply by offering something different.

At this point, though, you may be thinking, "But I'm *not* different. I just do acupuncture." Or massage. Or energy medicine. While that may be true, those are just the labels for what you do. Finding your real *difference* involves digging deeper.

Being different requires defining your offering in the context of others. When you say, "I'm an acupuncturist," you're talking about *you*. When you say, "Our clinic gives people an affordable way to get regular acupuncture treatments," you've changed the equation. You've given people that reason to choose you the first time and to *continue* to choose you after that.

It seems like a simple concept, but finding a difference that fits you and resonates with others can be a daunting task. Given the likely shortage of magical caves and glowing pools in your neighborhood, how do you find your crystal?

Stacey Weckstein and many others have found theirs with some expert help, and you might well do the same. But you can also find your difference on your own.

Sometimes, differences seem to come as standard equipment, built right in to practitioners. More often, though, they're discovered through the trial and error of being in daily practice. A difference is the unique intersection of creativity and practicality that's difficult to conjure up on demand. It's like sitting down with a blank pad of paper and a pen and telling yourself to think of a great invention or come up with a brilliant movie plot. It doesn't always work that way.

But there are clues we can follow in the paths of others on the journey. Consider these examples, and how they've found their crystals:

- For Andy Rosenfarb, specialization found him. He had a long history of eye issues, and after successfully helping himself, he began to help others. Over time, he learned more and found better results. Word spread, and his difference was put into action.

- Stacey Weckstein took some time off and found her difference by asking for help from a professional.
- Aranka Jones founded Sakura Naturopathic Medical Spa by focusing on her passion for beauty and healthy lifestyles.
- Lisa Rohler, founder of Working Class Acupuncture (more on WCA later), found her difference in her drive to make acupuncture affordable for a broader range of people. She now leads a movement of other clinicians looking to provide affordable treatments and a way to compete in crowded acupuncture markets.
- We found ours in patients' disillusionment with the service and results they received from the overloaded conventional care system.

Like these examples, there are many ways to find your difference. What's important to remember about creating your crystal is that it *will* happen if you feel it's important and if you commit to the idea of discovering it.

You don't, however, have to sit and wait. The best way to discover you difference is to look for traces of it in the clients, practices, and people around you, and in your own life and behaviors.

Other practices are a particularly helpful place to start. **There is no better way to find Success than to follow the trail of someone else.** An hour with a successful practitioner will teach you more than you might learn in years of practice. It doesn't mean copying them—your goal is simply to learn as much as possible about what works and what doesn't so you can shape your *own* difference in your own way.

If you feel uncertain about approaching other practitioners, don't worry—that's normal. But try to remember that almost everyone likes to be sincerely asked for advice. It's a compelling form of flattery. Very few people refuse, and almost no one is annoyed. If it makes you uncomfortable to approach practitioners where you already practice (or plan to practice), then just pick another town or city.

Here are some crystal-revealing questions you can ask yourself and others to help develop your own difference:

Ask yourself

Are there any health conditions I have unique experience with? Is there an aspect of health that I'm fanatical about? That I'll talk about to anyone who'll listen? Am I passionate about a specific condition, social issue, or business experience?

Ask other practitioners

Why do clients choose you? What do you love to do the most in your practice? Why do people choose you instead of finding the same service with another practitioner? Why do they stay with you? Or why not? What do you do or offer that people rave about the most? Is there anything that new clients ask for when they arrive because they've heard about it through word of mouth?

Ask your current clients

What brought you here? Why this practice and not another? What makes you stay? What do you love?

Ask non-clients

Have you ever considered <your modality>? If not, why not? If you have considered it but have never tried it, why haven't you tried it?

These questions tend to reveal glints of a practice crystal. Each provides an insight into what might attract and retain clients.

PUT YOUR DIFFERENCE TO THE TEST

You may not discover your difference right away. Crystals tend to build and become more powerful over time. But as your difference does begin to gel, you'll need to make sure that you're creating a crystal that actually works. Here are three things you need to know about your difference:

Crystal Test #1: Does your difference matter?

There are as many ways to define your difference as there are practitioners, but being different isn't the *whole* story. Your customers need to be able to distinguish your service as being superior in some way, but you also need to be offering something of value in the first place. In other words, a unique way of offering something that no one wants isn't a crystal that works for long.

It's one thing to be different. It's another to be different in the right way. For example, offering colon hydrotherapy at rock bottom prices might well be a way to differentiate, but in the end, it might not be a difference that customers care about. In fact, it may well be the opposite—people may actively *avoid* a discount pricing structure on elective procedures where their physical health is concerned. Your difference needs to be something that strikes a positive chord with people. It needs to resonate with them as being something they need. You may be the only practitioner in town with a martini bar in the waiting room, but is that what people *want?*

Your difference also needs to be something that can be explained. *You* might be able to define your difference, but can anyone else? The name of your profession, technique, or specific tool may be obvious to you, but does anyone else really understand what the labels homeopathy, ayurvedic, Bowen, or craniosacral mean? Whether it's you doing the defining or your website, brochure, or raving fans, your difference needs to be something that can be expressed and understood.

Sickness versus wellness

Many practitioners define their difference as "wellness." They promote prevention, for example, because it's an important part of their health care philosophy.

While it's an admirable approach (and there's no denying that wellness might just be the only philosophy that can get us out of our current health care crisis), wellness as a difference in your practice can be a hard sell. People don't want to find future wellness or prevent future problems. They want to resolve their *current illness*. It's the hard reality of health care: **people want to solve a current problem more than they want to prevent a future one.**

That doesn't mean you can't promote and deliver wellness and prevention—in fact, some practices depend on it—but many practitioners find it more effective to find new clients by focusing on a problem or an issue that prospective clients want to solve. Once you've attracted people to your practice, you can educate them on how to get and stay well. But in order to get them there in the first place and gain the trust necessary to promote wellness, you may need to meet people where they are: feeling anything *but* well.

Crystal Test #2: Does your difference matter to the right people?

You may have defined a difference that matters, but does it matter to the people it should?

It's tempting to believe that *any* client is a great client—especially when money's tight and every face that comes through the door is another chance to pay the rent.

But the truth is that you should be as selective in choosing your clients as your clients should be in choosing a doctor. Working with clients who fit well with you and your practice keep you happy, inspired, and energized. The "right" clients tend to respond well to your treatment, and that leads to more success. More success increases referrals (of similarly great clients) and the cycle continues.

A poor fit, on the other hand, does the opposite. It drains you of energy and generates poor results, which in turn sends an unhappy client out the door to complain about your service to their friends and colleagues.

Let's look at a few characteristics that all great clients share:

They comply

A client who can't (or won't) follow your advice is not likely to find success with your modality. This leads to the bad client spiral: no success = no return = no payment = no referral = negative publicity = less growth.

Clients need to buy in. They have to trust you and your experience, and they have to commit to following through—whether the process involves taking a supplement, getting a specific treatment, or making a difficult lifestyle change. No compliance, no success.

They pay

That may seem obvious, but clients who don't pay not only leave you cashless, our experience is that they also tend to get poorer results, leading to the same problems that you get when they don't comply. Do they have to be wealthy? No (unless that's part of your difference); but they do have to be able to pay your fees, whatever those may be.

They refer

In most practices, the bulk of new clients over time are going to come from referrals from existing clients. Clients who don't refer don't build your practice. That doesn't mean you don't want them. They're just not *ideal*.

You can help them

If you've been in practice for any length of time, then you know that there are some health conditions you're more likely to have success with than others. This success breeds more success in the form of positive word of mouth, referrals, increased confidence, and far greater satisfaction in practice. In other words, clients that you can help can also help you—either directly or indirectly.

And the ones you can't help? Learning when to say, "I don't think I can help you, but I know someone who can," is also a form of helping, and just as critical for growing a great client base.

They fit you

It may be tempting to grab every client you can, but remember that your success over time is going to happen through finding the best clients for your particular talent *and* your personality. Who do you click with? Who loves your style? In the end, loving your clients and their problems can make the difference between being excited to go to work and not being able to drag yourself out of bed in the morning.

Does every client have to be *ideal?* No, but the more clearly you define who you want in your practice, the more effectively you can use your time, energy, and financial resources to find them.

Don't underestimate the power of having a clear vision of your ideal client. A vision delivers a certain confidence that comes from knowing what to do next. There's a sense of momentum that builds as you move toward a clear goal—in this case, attracting and retaining the clients who are right for you. Defining your ideal client can energize you in ways you might not have imagined. If you've always been turned off by the idea of marketing and networking, then you might be pleasantly surprised at how effortless (and yes, even enjoyable) it seems when you have a clear vision.

Still, at this point you're likely thinking that the odds of you saying "no" to someone are pretty slim. Unless you're currently overbooked or seeking some balance, this probably looks like one of those ideas that you pay lip service to.

We agree—you're not likely to say "no" to anyone. At least, not at first. But the objective here is not to say "no" to what we don't want, but to put our focus on what we *do* want. We don't want to say "no" to more of the wrong clients—we want to say "yes" to more of the *right* ones. The more clients we have who are a great fit, the more success we'll have, and the more we'll tend to see more clients just like them.

Creating that vision of an ideal client is about saying "yes," not "no." It's about seeking those to include (not exclude) and being able to describe that ideal client visit to others. Why define a difference that matters to the people you can't help, or don't want to?

When we move to the next chapter, it becomes even more important to know your target market. Spending time, money, and energy on marketing you and your practice to the wrong people can be a frustrating and expensive process. What's worse, it can trap you in Getting By or on a tour of Burnout en route to No Longer Practicing. Either way, it leads to nowhere you want to be.

Crystal Test #3: Does your difference matter to enough people?

There's another critical factor in defining your difference: *the people your difference matters to actually have to exist.*

Just as too broad a definition can leave you floating aimlessly or give you a practice full of clients you can't connect with, creating too narrow a description of your ideal client can reduce your target market to a very small number of clients who can't support your practice. Tamara Hutchins discovered that her facial rejuvenation niche was shrinking and she needed to broaden her appeal to attract more people (which, in turn, delivered more people to her specialty). Restricting yourself to female athletes with anxiety issues, for example, might be too narrow a difference unless you have a large population base to draw on.

How many clients are enough? It's going to vary depending on your profession, your hours, the cost of operating your clinic, how you run your business, and your own definition of your needs. The easiest way to find out how many clients you might need is to find a busy practitioner whose practice is similar to yours and simply ask.

HOW TO SUSTAIN YOUR DIFFERENCE

It can be difficult to hold onto your difference. Someone else can become the best, or offer the same service, or become the cheapest, or specialize in the same thing you do. In short, someone can make your difference *their* difference, which would leave both of you less, well, different.

How do you deal with this? After all, it'd be reassuring if you could pour your heart and soul into differentiating yourself without feeling like all your hard work might be swept away from you.

The good thing is that you can find your difference *and* sustain it, too. Here's how.

Have multiple differences

Can you be the cheapest *and* the best? Can you be the only practitioner to offer system X *and* provide the best service in town? Can you be the only specialist in town working with athletes *and* be the cheapest *and* provide the best service?

The answer is no. At least, not *always*. But if you can support multiple differences that make sense, then go for it. Can you be the cheapest and provide the most luxurious high-end boutique service? Perhaps not, but you might be able to be the cheapest and offer the best customer service if you put your mind to it.

Widen the gap

So yes, you can have *more* differences. But what about the *quantity* of that difference? You can be the cheapest by a penny, but that's not much of a difference. You can provide just a little bit more than the next practitioner, but a little bit isn't much.

Can you be the best by 100 percent? By 1,000 percent? Can you offer twice as much for the same price? Twice as much for half the price? Two unique services instead of one? How about four? Can you specialize in something but also be price competitive? Can you be so incredibly good that you're not only the best, but your "bestness" is so remarkable (and therefore unchallengeable) that it amazes?

The *more* different you are, the better you can sustain and defend your difference. The brighter the crystal, the better it works and the longer it lasts.

Build a brand

During a recent trip to a place we'll call "Anytown" (try inserting the name of your town or city and following along), we noticed that the local massage therapy business, "Anytown Massage," had been spending some serious marketing dollars on advertising—everything from newspaper ads, glossy magazine spreads, and posters to a brand new sign in front of the practice. At a children's birthday party at the bowling alley, we noticed that it had sponsored lanes, so that each time the pins were set up, a banner proclaiming "Anytown Massage" was revealed.

We read the fine print on some of the ads because we were curious from a business perspective. What Anytown Massage had to say was actually pretty helpful. It described why it was different, and it seemed to be able to solve some serious health problems.

Good for them for trying, but Anytown Massage spent a lot of good money in a bad way.

First of all, the ads were simply "Anytown Massage" in capital letters with no distinguishing logo, no specialized font, no icon, no slogan, not even any color. Not terribly memorable.

Furthermore, when you live in Anytown, the name itself becomes essentially meaningless. There's an Anytown Garage and an Anytown Flea Market. There's an Anytown Drugstore and an Anytown Cinema. Without the addition of some kind of distinguishing marketing feature, the Anytown ads do one thing: *They tell potential clients that they should consider massage therapy in their town.*

But isn't that good? You might think so, since massage therapy can be helpful for many people suffering from a wide range of issues. The problem, however, is that it's not helping *Anytown Massage.* It's helping the citizens of Anytown, and it's helping the local massage industry, but there's no guarantee that it's helping Anytown Massage specifically.

Even if they were recommended to us by the highest authority, there's a good chance we wouldn't be able to pluck them out of the yellow pages the next time we needed a massage. The thousands of dollars they spent on advertising might convince us to get a much-needed treatment, but the odds aren't great that it would be from them.

Anytown Massage lacks a brand. They have a generic name that describes what they do and where they do it. That's it. And without some kind of unique visual identifier like a logo, they're doing nothing but increasing awareness of massage therapy in the region of Anytown.

In reality, Anytown Massage is likely doing okay, but it's in spite of themselves. They're trying hard, and as a result they're probably getting new clients from sheer effort, but they're only getting a fraction of what they should be for all that time and money.

Every single Anytown Massage advertising dollar has a good chance of driving business to another massage therapist. In fact, Anytown Massage would do far better with a name based on a town in *another time zone* than they will with their own town's name. "Palm Springs Massage Therapy," for example, would probably do better in Nebraska than in Palm Springs itself. At least there it would be different.

The lesson here is that it's hard to defend a generic name and image. When the clinic down the street comes up with an infrared sauna or some fancy new massage system, it'll be easier to compete if you've got a strong brand.

Build a relationship

A brand is more than just a logo, however. It's a symbol of the relationship you have with your clients. When your clients trust you and what you offer because of the relationship you've carefully built with them, then they stick with you.

That relationship, however, is more than just the exchange of their money for your services. Relationships require something more. When a clients says, for example, "It's okay to contact me" (whether it be by email, phone, mail, or any other medium), then they're giving you an advantage—a way to keep your difference in front of them at your discretion. The relationship has expanded beyond simple commerce. When you go the extra mile for a client, you've done more than process a credit card payment—you've fostered trust and patronage.

The stronger and longer the relationship with your clients, the harder it is for them to leave to go elsewhere and the farther they spread your difference by word of mouth.

Always be changing

Or, more accurately, always be *improving*. Most differences are easy to copy. When you get treatment tool X, someone else can easily buy the newer model Y. If you add weekend hours, so can your competition.

What's hard to duplicate is the energy and ideas of a practice that is willing to continually improve. Adopting the belief of constantly improving from the previous chapter not only works wonders for your practice, but it also makes it difficult for others to keep up.

Can you offer the same old thing as someone else and still survive? The answer is yes, provided that what you offer is valuable and you don't mind skirting the edges of No Longer Practicing. In fact, offering something of value is critical, and we're assuming that you have something people want. So yes, you could skip all this "be different" stuff and just hang out your wellness shingle. However, if you want to grow your practice at a decent rate, to a decent size, pay yourself a decent salary, be able to thrive during periods of competition, and perhaps even sell your practice one day at a price tag that reflects your hard work, then you need to take finding your difference seriously.

Don't gloss over this idea of defining your difference. When times get tough or you're facing complicated decisions, having a clear "big-picture" vision of your practice, what it offers, and how it's different will make things much easier.

Take the time to dig into your vision of your practice. What are you best at? What are you passionate about? What do you hate? What do your clients love the most about you? What do you love the most about them? Somewhere in that passion lie the seeds of your difference.

And what if you don't have a difference? Don't worry—it just means you haven't found your crystal *yet*. You don't need to shut your doors (or delay getting started) while you decide. As Andy Rosenfarb said about finding a specialty, "Decide to specialize, even if you do not know what you want to specialize in. For now, just be clear in your mind that you desire to be a leading author-ity in *something*."

Andy may have been speaking about focusing on a specific health issue, but the point applies far more broadly. be clear in your mind that you *need* to be different, and the difference will come.

BEYOND THE CAVE

The cave is the first of the four challenges in private practice. Of all the pitfalls on the path to Success, it's the hardest to recognize and also the one responsible for the most failed practices. It's the most abstract barrier on the path, but also the most pervasive, bleeding into every aspect of your daily routine.

Sure, there are a number of other things that *seem* like the reason practices fail. You might argue that practices fail because they don't attract new clients. Or that the practitioners fail to keep those clients. But when practitioners are in the cave, client numbers aren't causes, they're *symptoms*. They're signs that practitioners have failed to fill a gap in their beliefs or in their understanding of their practices.

Like any symptom, client numbers can be treated (as we'll see), but if you're stuck in the dark, unaware of what's missing, then you'll be treating symptoms forever, never reaching the root of the problem. You need to leave the cave to truly move ahead on the path.

Tamara Hutchins, the acupuncturist whose story started this section, needed to look first at her reflection in the pool to realize that she was lacking some fundamental business skills. She then had to work on her crystal. Her original difference, a specialization in facial rejuvenation acupuncture, wasn't serving her in a changing economy. Donning her business hat and broadening her reach led her out of the cave, and created a new flow of clients and new levels of success.

The reason we find ourselves in the cave in our story is not dissimilar from the way we find ourselves in trouble in practice: by rushing ahead and forgetting the fundamentals. In practice, the predicament of the cave is made worse by the fact that most of us don't even realize we're there. The light has been dimming so slowly for so long that we haven't even noticed. What makes the cave so challenging is that *we don't know what we don't know.* It's easy to count new clients. It's easy to check our bank balances. But no one tells us, "You know, I think the way you're *thinking* about your practice is keeping you from becoming successful."

How do you know when you're facing the cave? Here are a few warning signs that you may be lost in the dark and not realize it:

- You know your clinical skills are excellent, but you're losing existing clients or failing to attract new ones.
- You don't understand the financial health of your practice.
- You actively ignore financial concerns in your practice.
- You're not moving ahead with your practice because you're waiting to make one giant, sweeping change that will make a huge difference.
- You're losing interest in your practice.
- You feel guilty or unsure about telling clients your rates.
- You regularly discount your fees, offer freebies when you shouldn't, or fail to collect on accounts that are past due.
- You feel like you have too many competitors who are eating away at your client base and making it harder and harder for you to find new clients.

- You have a tough time creating marketing materials that deliver results.
- You can't easily and succinctly describe how your practice is different from that of another practitioner in the same profession.
- You seem to be able to attract attention to your practice, but people seem to choose someone else instead of you.
- You use statements like, "I just want to help people with their health, not worry about all that business stuff" or "I don't worry about the money side of things."

Each of these sentiments is a sign of the challenge of the cave—either a lack of insight or knowledge in you, the practitioner, or a lack of difference in your practice. Each will continue to cause problems until they are resolved by understanding and developing yourself (the pool) or understanding and developing your unique practice (the crystal).

Make no mistake: each practitioner experiences her own cave. It's that stretch of unease that leaves us uncertain as to how to proceed, or makes us second-guess our skills and future in a healing profession. For some, the cave is a one-time occurrence. For others, there are many dark stretches on the road to Success. The cave might come early in practice or, as it did for Tamara, it might arrive unexpectedly after many successful years.

Regardless of how deep, dark, or confusing the cave may be, know that there is a way out. The pool and the crystal are powerful tools for lighting your way. They help build a solid foundation for your practice by acknowledging that how you *think* about your practice is the most fundamental part of the journey to Success. Their message is straightforward: get your head on straight, create something you love that enough people can find value in, and you're on your way.

In the end, of course, what we all discover is that the cave is really a *tunnel.* It's a stretch of darkness that's necessary to pass through in order to continue on the path, and it *does* have an end. What's most important to remember is that you can't find your way through without simply moving forward. Staying in the darkness and wishing things were different won't get you any closer to the exit. If you don't know what to do next, or if you're having trouble defining your difference, then commit to doing *something* with the idea that if it doesn't work, you'll at least have eliminated one side tunnel in the maze of the dark cave.

Once you do leave the cave—and you will—the question becomes what to do next. Once you've adopted the mindset you need in order to move forward on the path, and once you've created something of value, how do you get people to embrace it?

For that we need to head back to the path.

INSIGHTS FROM THE CAVE

The cave represents a gap in your understanding of yourself or your practice—a blank spot on the map of the journey—and is the single biggest reason most practices fail.

THE POOL

Continuing your personal development beyond clinical skills is critical to practice success.

THE CRYSTAL

Finding your unique difference helps you make better decisions, and more easily attract and retain clients.

PART II: THE RIVER
Attracting New Clients

You drown not by falling into a river, but by staying submerged in it.

-Paulo Coelho

ith the darkness and uncertainty of the cave behind you, you strike out on the path. You're relieved to be back on track and excited to push ahead. To your right is a river, winding its way through the trees, and as far as you can tell, the path more or less follows its meandering course.

As you settle into your pace, your mind drifts back to the message of the cave. You feel the hard edges of the crystal in your pocket, and for the first time you realize something: *you're alone.* The forest sounds of chirping birds and rustling leaves surround you and the river rushes noisily past, but there's no sign of any *people.*

You recall the message at the beginning of the path: *help as many people along the way as you can.* You're anxious to get started. But where is everyone? How will you find success as a healer if there's no one to heal?

Just as you begin to wonder whether your journey will end before it's hardly even begun, you smell smoke on the breeze. *People,* you think, and you pick up the pace. The smell of smoke grows stronger as you push forward, and before long you catch the scent of cooking, too. Sure enough, you soon spy rooftops through gaps in the trees. You must be getting close.

Your suspicions are confirmed when you round a bend in the path and see a small town in the distance. Hundreds, maybe thousands of people head to and fro, going about their daily lives. Your spirits soar. You'll soon have all the people you need!

As you draw closer, you once again pull the crystal from your pocket. In the sunshine it seems to explode into a million bright shards of light. True to the message of the cave, the talisman has an almost immediate effect, and several heads begin to turn in your direction. *It's working!* you think.

There's just one problem.

The meandering river you've been following has changed. It's grown, and its cold water is pouring over slippery rocks to create a thundering roar. It's an impressive sight, but daunting to approach. You look ahead, where the path and river disappear into the distance. The good news is that as far as you can tell, the path stays on your side of the river so you won't have to cross it to continue your journey.

The bad news is that everyone else is on the other side.

Standing on the path, you're completely separated from every person you might be able to help by a torrent of dark, rushing water.

Fortunately, though, the crystal is still shining. Drawn by its glow, a few curious onlookers move closer to the riverbank. Encouraged by their interest, you wave to catch their attention but the river is so daunting that they turn and move on.

After some time, yet another passerby draws closer. This time you shout, but the river is too loud for her to hear. She too takes one look at the swift current, then moves on.

The same thing continues for hours. Even when you *do* manage to catch people's attention and motion for them to join you on your side of the river, they take one look at the cold water, shake their heads, and then move on with their lives.

You consider crossing to the other side yourself, but you wonder how you'll continue to follow the path to Success if you leave this side of the river.

Finally, after pacing the path for several hours, you realize that until you find a way to get some people across the river, you'll be alone and Success will remain out of reach.

✳

Right now, you're a professional in one of the most important, fastest-growing industries in the world. Around the globe, health care is sliding into crisis mode, and conventional care is having trouble keeping up. Aging populations, overloaded systems, and ineffective solutions are driving people to seek options.

Those options are *you*. While it can be a troubling time to be a health care consumer, there really has never been a better time to be a practitioner. There are probably enough clients within a few miles of your office to fill a dozen new practices. In fact, there are likely thousands of potential clients who could all use CAM care that live within *walking* distance of most clinics.

So why aren't more of them showing up in your practice?

It's a strange paradox. Despite the demand for health care, practitioners are struggling. Everywhere we look there are people in desperate need of better health, but for some reason we can't seem to get enough of them to our practices. Even when we've defined our difference and created something of true value for people, it often seems, as one practitioner told us, "As if something prevents people from taking that big first step of walking through the door."

It turns out that there *is* something stopping people. It's what we call the *river*, and it's a barrier that prevents people from taking the final step toward becoming a client.

In the figurative world of our story, the river is a physical barrier with its swift current, freezing water, and slippery rocks. Crossing it is too uncertain, too scary. People may well *want* to cross, but the whole thing just seems too risky.

In the real world of your practice, the barriers may be less visible but they're equally as daunting. Cost, ease of access, misinformation, uncertainty and lack of trust are less tangible, but no less powerful obstacles that stop potential clients from becoming *actual* ones.

The river is the uncertainty that keeps people from becoming clients. To attract more clients to your practice, your job is to get people across the river—to make the risks less risky and the uncertainties more certain.

The water's edge: Why advertising isn't everything

Most of us tackle the river by instinct. To encourage people to cross, we advertise our services. In essence, we stand on our side of the river and wave our arms frantically shouting, "Notice me! I'm over here!" The trouble is that the river can be wide and the water loud. People don't always notice us. And in most cases we're not the only ones waving and shouting—after all, there are plenty of others competing for attention.

And it's not just other practitioners that we're competing with. The noise of everyday life—work, families, bills, overloaded schedules, and a million other modern-day distractions—makes the world a busy place. A place where attention is in limited supply.

Faced with all this competition, our natural tendency is to try *harder*. We jump up and down on the shore and we shout as loudly as we can. Sometimes we wade right into the water so we can drag people back with us by promising them the moon. Instead of finding new clients, though, we often find our integrity washing down the river and we end up wet, cold, and no further ahead than when we started.

All that jumping, waving, and shouting is just the same old marketing. It's our attempt to be heard above the noise and hubbub of daily life. Traditional print advertisements like newspaper ads, postcards, and flyers. Media spots like radio and TV ads. They're the equivalent of standing on the edge of the river and shouting. Newer mediums like online advertising and websites? More shouting and more jumping up and down.

Eventually, all that shouting and jumping up and down *will* get you clients—particularly if you're a good shouter. But in the end, only a fraction of the clients in a busy practice are delivered solely by advertising. It might get people to the shore, but most turn away at that point.

Advertising doesn't get many people across the river. It just gets them to the water's edge.

The problem is that most practitioners don't distinguish between getting someone's *attention* (shouting) and turning that someone into a *client* (helping them cross the river). Understanding that distinction is what differentiates practices that grow quickly from the ones that inch forward.

The next two chapters explain the key strategies for helping people not only to reach the water's edge, but to actually cross the river to your practice. Follow these two key strategies and you'll have no shortage of new companions on the path to Success.

3. Stepping Stones

No one tests the depth of a river with both feet.

-African Proverb

eather Furby, certified massage therapist and founder of Body Logic, faces an ongoing challenge in her California practice.

"The bodywork industry in northern California is *very* crowded," she told us. "We have an inordinate number of day spas due to the tourism of the Sonoma and Napa Valleys. The massage super chains have found a home in our cities. In addition, the certification in California is a mere 100 hours. After that, one is free to use the CMT label."

To make things even more challenging, California attracts an abundance of energy healers and other related practitioners. The market is saturated. There are, in other words, a lot of practitioners in northern California shouting and waving their arms. And because the state has few licensing requirements, there are few professional standards—it's easy for consumers to be disappointed or wary. In California, the river is fast and wide, and potential clients are not easily duped into getting wet for no good reason.

Despite these challenges, though, Heather's found a way to get clients across the river: she educates them. Heather's first appointment with a client isn't a massage. It's a free 15- to 30-minute phone call where she carefully listens to their needs and then explains exactly what Body Logic offers and how it's different.

It may seem like an unusual first step for a massage therapist, but Heather's offering isn't a typical relaxation massage. Body Logic is a unique approach to pain, trauma, and injury designed to align what she calls the physical, emotional, cognitive, and spiritual *bodies*. The 15- to 30-minute phone session is time well spent because it gives clients a complete understanding of what Body Logic offers and how it can help. By the end of the call, the potential client knows Heather and has a very good idea of whether or not she can help. By that point, the prospect has either become a client or has been carefully referred to another therapist for care. In either case, that person is being gently helped across the river.

Crossing the river is tricky business. As a practitioner, you crossed over long ago. You know the river—its currents, drop offs, and slippery spots are old news to you. You can cross the river with your eyes closed without getting so much as a wet sock. Of course, that's because you've already bought into your philosophy; you've already embraced your methodology. You understand the benefit of what you do so well that it seems crazy to you that *everyone* isn't crossing the river. For you, there's no risk.

Not so for your prospective clients. For them, choosing a health care provider or a treatment modality isn't always so easy, and the vast majority of them don't make the leap without a good look at the bank on the other side. In fact, most of them don't leap at *all*.

People don't like to leap. Many are too uncertain to go from "non-client" to "client" in one step. While you might drive down the street, decide on a whim that you need a bite to eat, and stop at the next grocery store, the average person deliberates a little longer when making health care decisions—particularly if it involves something new. For most people, there's at least one step between being a complete stranger and becoming a client.

As author and marketing guru Seth Godin notes:

> *Do you really expect that the first time we transact, it will involve me giving you money in exchange for a product or service?*
>
> *Perhaps this is a good strategy for a pretzel vendor on the street, but is that the best you can hope for?*
>
> *...I can watch a video. I can engage in a conversation. We can connect, transfer knowledge, engage in a way that builds trust... all of these things make it more likely that I'll trust you enough to send you some money one day....*
>
> *But send you money on the first date? No way.* [2]

That "first date" is the step between prospect and client. For Heather, the first date is that 15-minute phone call. It's where potential clients decide whether or not the risk of crossing the river is worth it. **To help them make that step, your job is to reduce the risk.**

There are many risks. The cost of treatment. Potential side effects. The disapproval of others (including other health professionals). The time commitments. They're the downsides of becoming a client, and if (like the river) they rise to a certain level, prospects won't cross over. The challenge, of course, is that we can't reduce many of these risks in the long run. We can't always lower the cost of treatment or change how a family doctor feels about an alternative modality.

What we can do, however, is control three unknowns:

Unknown #1: People don't know you're there

Often, many prospective clients simply aren't aware you exist. They have no idea that on the other side of the river is a wonderful CAM practitioner just waiting to help them feel better.

Unknown #2: They don't know you personally

Health care is personal stuff, particularly in the CAM professions. Although they might know you're out there, they don't have the personal connection with you to trust you or feel comfortable entering into a health care relationship with you.

Unknown #3: They don't know you can help

The people on the other side of the river may know you're there, but they don't realize that you can help them with their specific problems. *A holistic nutritionist? Well, I'm sure she's lovely, but she couldn't possibly help with my skin issues.*

People who aren't yet your customers don't realize the value of what you offer. They don't know how great you are or how great you are at what you do. They don't know if they like you yet. They don't realize that you're sane, safe, credible, and sensible. Most important, they have yet to discover *why paying you is going to help them.* The three barriers above are like the swift current, slippery rocks, and freezing cold water. They represent the main risks of crossing the river. Your practice may be warm, dry, and safe, but any single one of the barriers above will stop a number of people from finding that out. Any two will stop a lot of people. And all three will stop everyone.

The key to being able to help the people at the water's edge— that is, to turn that unrealized mass of prospects into clients—is to add a stepping stone between "non-client" and "client." Instead of convincing those non-clients to go the whole distance and become clients in your practice, we're going to convince them to just *come one step closer*, in effect creating a "stepping stone" that gets them partway across the river.

Those stepping stones are like little islands in the stream. They help the curious take a first step and the indifferent begin to think, "Maybe this *could* help me."

A stepping stone is something that allows people to have a more intimate experience with you and your practice with little or no risk. Stepping stones get people into the river without getting them wet. And if we can get people closer and closer to our side of the river while ensuring that they still feel safe, stable, and secure, then the risk of the final leap will eventually be small enough to take.

FINDING YOUR STEPPING STONES

In the real world where your prospective clients aren't actually crossing a rushing river to reach your door, what does a stepping stone look like? What's the real-world equivalent of the island in the stream?

Here are a few examples of stepping stones you can use to get people a little closer to your side of the river:

Stepping stone #1: Information sessions

Information sessions are free group gatherings where practitioners can give a short presentation to the public. They can be done in your office or in a public space. Generally, info sessions are best attended when they're geared toward a specific condition or benefit. "Come and learn about acupuncture," for example, isn't as effective as "Five effective solutions for chronic pain."

Information sessions take some time to prepare for at first, but they get easier and they also allow you to connect with multiple prospects at the same time. That means you can reach more people with less time and effort.

Stepping stone #2: Speaking engagements

Every town or city has innumerable support groups, service clubs, associations, and professional groups that regularly invite guest speakers to address their members and the public at large. If you don't mind speaking to a group, it's a great way to entice a few people into the river to discover just how helpful crossing over can be.

Don't be scared off by the idea that this is a "speaking engagement." You don't need to be a public speaking rock star to pull this off. It's simply an opportunity to talk about what you know and are passionate about.

Don't feel like you're begging for favors here. In every community there are people right now who've been tasked with finding a speaker for their next business luncheon, club breakfast, or social night. You'd be doing *them* a huge favor if you'd be their guest.

Stepping stone #3: Free services

Nothing says "put your money where your mouth is" like offering what you do for free. If your service is truly of value, why not let people try it and see for themselves?

There are some obvious advantages to this. People can experience the real service as it's normally delivered with absolutely no risk beyond their time. It's a great way to convert skeptics and fence-sitters.

But there are also some drawbacks. Some modalities take a while to take effect; one free visit with no impact is going to make people feel like it's not worth paying for. It also takes time out of your day. If your service requires lengthy appointments, then too many freebies can eat up a schedule pretty quickly. And besides, even clients who are already willing to pay will often choose to take the free service first. That means that you end up eating a lot more free visits than you should.

Free services tend to work best when:

- There's immediate impact from one visit. If it takes several visits to make a difference for someone, you might be better off trying Body Logic's 15-minute approach, which doesn't leave people with a "tried it but nothing happened" sensation.
- You can work in groups (yoga or fitness classes, for example) where the cost of adding an extra person to the group is extremely low.
- You're confident that your service is one that lends itself to repeat visits so that you can be reasonably sure of getting back your investment.

Stepping stone #4: Limited trials

For membership-type services such as health clubs, yoga studios, or spa centers, a free trial membership that lasts for a limited time can be a great way to attract new faces.

The upside for most membership-based services is that the cost to offer a trial is relatively low. Adding one more person to a group is often inexpensive. The only caveat here is that what you offer has to be good—with a free trial, people are getting to sample the whole enchilada, and if they don't like what they try then they're not likely to continue.

Stepping stone #5: Digital islands

Nutrition and lifestyle counselor Andrea Ramirez has never advertised her practice. But she constantly offers stepping stones. On her website you can sign up for a free email course on how to eat well and live passionately, which also includes audio of Andrea speaking. You can subscribe to her blog, or connect with her via any number of social networking tools. You can subscribe to her *Nourishing News* newsletter or join her True Nourishment Divas' Group. And you can do it all for free.

If you have no idea who Andrea is, what she does, or how she can help, you can find out without so much as standing up from your desk. You can see her smiling face, hear her voice, and understand her approach. You can even connect with her clients. In short, if you want to get to know Andrea, you can cross the river without taking a single step.

The digital world isn't just paper transferred to screen. Podcasts, streaming video, newsletters, social media—and who knows what else by the time you read this—they all offer a whole new way to get clients across the river. The best part is that these stepping stones are nearly free and unbelievably more powerful than words in a brochure. They offer the next best thing to an intimate, in-person experience.

There are drawbacks, though. "It takes longer online," Andrea said. "When someone is looking for a counselor, they're looking for someone they can trust." So for the times when the internet just doesn't get people all the way across the river, Andrea reaches out directly in workshops, cooking classes, and other in-person stepping stones.

Stepping stone #6: Free products

If you sell products as well as services, offering a freebie can be an effective stepping stone to getting people in the door. It has a few downsides, though: a great free product can be expensive and attract a lot of people who are only interested in the freebie itself. Conversely, a lousy giveaway doesn't attract anyone. Free products probably produce the lowest percentage of "qualified" prospects (people who are legitimate candidates for what you offer), but they can compensate by bringing more faces in the door.

Stepping stone #7: Gifts

Unlike free services (which are products and trials that you as the practitioner give to prospects), *gifts* are opportunities for your *clients* to provide a stepping stone for the people in their lives who they think might benefit from your services.

Gifts can be paid for by the giver—things like gift certificates are a great example—or they can be paid for by the practitioner and dispensed by the giver. A good example of this is a "bring a friend" or "buy one get one" promotion that allows an existing client to offer your services to someone new at no extra charge to the client or the prospect.

Both approaches work, and both allow your current clients to easily share your value with others.

Stepping stone #8: The 15-minute solution

For some professions—and some professionals—giving away free services isn't the preferred option. For us, it tended to invite the kind of clients we weren't looking for—the ones who had difficulty making tough lifestyle changes or continuing through long courses of treatment.

If you can't (or won't) offer a free service, though, you're still faced with the same challenge of getting people to take their first steps into the river—particularly in terms of prospects getting to know you personally and finding out if you can help.

Providing a brief "get to know me" session (15 minutes is usually enough time) takes care of both of those challenges in a low-risk way. Prospective clients get to connect with you in person, and at the same time discover whether you can help them with their unique health care challenges. It's the Body Logic approach, and it can work wonders.

The complimentary "meet the practitioner" visit is also an easy sell for staff. If you have front desk support, they can easily answer any question by simply saying, "Why don't you come in for a free appointment? It's an easy way to get your questions answered." It also makes it easy for clients, colleagues, friends, and other referring sources to direct possible clients your way—after all, it's no risk to them either.

If you're concerned about giving away 15 minutes of free time, consider the following:

- Most of the people who take you up on the 15-minute offer are likely to be people who wouldn't use your service *without* this option. It tends to attract those unsure people who might make great clients, but wouldn't make a move without the personal connection or the confidence that you can help.
- You're investing 15 minutes for perhaps many years of patronage and referrals.
- Conversion is likely to be high. Unless you've got some serious interpersonal challenges, many of your 15-minute visitors are likely to become clients.

Learning to use this as our primary offering has made a massive difference in our new client numbers. The cost is low, the conversion is high, and it also lets us more accurately find the clients who really fit.

Stepping stone #9: Partnerships

Not all stepping stones need to be your own. Another practitioner in a related field may well be using these same tools. So why not partner? There's no reason a yoga instructor, a nutritionist, and a homeopath can't combine forces to offer information on a condition like fibromyalgia or on a topic like healthy parenting.

The great thing about partnerships is that they help build a critical mass of people to participate in things like information sessions. Nothing attracts attention like 50 or 60 people wading into a river at the same time.

Stepping stone #10: Your difference

Your difference is a powerful stepping stone. Figuratively speaking, a brightly shining crystal is often enough on its own to convince people to move closer to the river. A vibrant difference gets attention, and attention attracts people closer to you. Often, it attracts them close enough to cross right over. When you're the "go-to" source for a service or product, the river tends to appear much less daunting to prospective clients.

MAKING YOUR STEPPING STONES WORK

Some stepping stones can be a lot of effort, and it's important to only use the ones that work. You might offer a wide variety of stepping stones in your practice, but if very few people actually cross the river completely and become clients, then you're wasting a lot of time and money for no good reason. Taking the time to place those rocks in the current and working to get people to step onto them is only worth the effort if enough people truly decide to cross to the other side.

Here are a few strategies for ensuring that those people who come part way to you decide to make the final step and become your client:

Cover the three unknowns

Your stepping stones need to deal with the three key unknowns that your clients face: knowing you exist, knowing you personally, and knowing you can help. Not every form of stepping stone covers all three, and not every client needs to be reassured on all counts. To make sure you're covering the variety of unknowns and client personalities, and to get the most from the stepping stone strategy in your practice, you'll need to ensure you've got your bases covered. Make certain that your risk-free opportunities for potential clients answer the following questions:

- Can people easily gain as much information as possible about your services without taking a risk?
- Are there ways for people to get to know you personally without assuming any risk?
- Is there a way for people to know that you can help with their specific health care problems?
- Do you have a stepping stone that's always available? Things like information sessions and speaking engagements might be irregular events, but a 15-minute appointment at the prospect's convenience is a stepping stone that's more accessible. Better still, digital stepping stones are available 24-7.

You may find that you need more than one stepping stone to cover the three "knows." In our practice, we used these key strategies to ensure that potential clients could wade into the river without risk:

- A complimentary 15-minute "meet the doctor" visit.
- Occasional info sessions and speaking gigs—once per month maximum.
- A comprehensive website with a long FAQ section, including lists of conditions and complaints that we help with, as well as regular free updates by email and various social platforms.
- Clarifying key barriers in person and on our website.
- Well-trained staff with great product knowledge who know to offer the 15-minute visit to anyone who seems unsure.
- Adding specific conditions to our print and online advertising.
- Adding the "meet the doctor" visit to our advertising.

Why so many stepping stone strategies, you might ask? Every client is unique, and the river—the gap between you and them—looks different to everyone. Some people need one simple stepping stone—a tiny bit of information, perhaps—while others need more. Confidence means something different to everyone, and multiple stepping stones give you a better chance of finding the one that's going to bring someone closer to you.

Market your stepping stones

Marketers will tell you to "sell the sizzle, not the steak" or to "talk benefits, not features," and it's true—your marketing, regardless of its medium, needs to provide some reason for people to consider you. The challenge, though, is that in this day and age, people are more media savvy. You can claim all the benefits you like, but in the end, people are far more skeptical towards marketing than they used to be.

This is health care. It's important, it's intimate, and it's often expensive. The stakes are high, and people need more than marketing copy; they need to try it themselves. They need to get close and have a look. They need to get into the river so they can see what's on the other side more clearly and realize that what you've been shouting over the river's roar is actually the real deal.

When it comes to your marketing, push the stepping stones. Yes, do all the other great things you're supposed to do in advertising, but make sure you offer the entry point into the river.

Advertising strategies such as print ads, flyers, postcards, billboards, and online ads often target only one "know"—helping people know you exist—and they cost more money than many stepping stones. If you do use them, make sure you mention one of your other stepping stones so that your potential clients can see the next step to getting across the river.

Our new client numbers really took off when we started marketing our 15-minute complimentary visits. We'd always offered the option, but once we started *promoting* it, the phone *really* started ringing. There was a big difference between saying, "We can help with condition X," and saying, "Drop by and we'll tell you for free just exactly how we can."

Once we got someone in the door, they almost always became a client. And if we didn't think we could help, we could often find someone who *could*. Even now we continue to get referrals from people who aren't even clients but who still had a great stepping stone experience.

Create a clear plan

Prospects who use stepping stones are naturally more cautious than those who just jump right into your practice as a full-fledged client. It's been our experience that those people have a strong need to understand the big picture of your practice and how it works. To win them over to your side, make sure you paint a picture of the entire treatment plan, including what the objective is, how long it will take to reach it, how they'll know when they reach it, and how they'll feel along the way.

If someone has a skin rash, for example, which one of these approaches is going to encourage them to take the next step?

> *I think we can help with that. Let's get you booked in for an appointment later this week.*

Or

> *We should be able to reduce this rash almost, if not entirely, back to normal. We'll do three weeks of x, including some y that should reduce the itch. We'll see some improvement within the first two weeks, and if we don't, we'll reassess.*

The clear plan with easily identifiable outcomes makes it straightforward for clients to comply and also creates the confidence that people need to commit. Remember—*people have to believe you can help.*

Get permission to stay in touch

Not everyone is going to become a client the moment they use one of your stepping stones. Some people need time to decide, while others need multiple stepping stones to get them close enough to your side of the river to finally make the leap. Sometimes, their need simply isn't great enough to follow through at that moment.

Those people who come part way and then turn back are not a complete loss, however. They could become a client in the future, and now that you've ensured they know you exist, it's important to get their permission to connect with them again in the future.

The easiest way to do this is via email or another digital contact tool. You can leverage each stepping stone—whether it's a one-on-one discussion, an online FAQ, or a speaking engagement—by collecting email addresses. It takes only a moment to pass around a signup form to a group of people, and adding one to your website is easier than you think.

From there, it's relatively easy (and cheap) to send out an email newsletter to your list. (For some easy tools to help you create and distribute your online newsletter, visit our website at practitionersjourney.com.)

Focus on solutions, not treatments

You'll get your best conversion rates when you focus on the benefit to the client rather than on the treatment itself. It's not about the personalized nutrition plan, it's about how designing something just right for the client is going to make his life easier and help him feel better. It's not about the chiropractic adjustment, it's about what the adjustment will do for his migraines.

In short, it's not about *you* at all. It's about how your client will *feel* after you apply your solution.

Address risks and barriers

Beyond the three "knows"—knowing you're there, knowing you personally, and knowing you can help—there are innumerable tiny barriers that might be preventing a prospect from becoming a client. In our 15-minute sessions and our marketing material, we do our best to address any remaining barriers that might still stand in the way of someone becoming a client. How much will it cost? Will we work with their medical doctors? How long will it take? Can they use what we offer and still take their medication? The 15-minute session lets us reduce the river to a mere trickle.

Tout your experience

People love to be in capable hands, and nothing says "capable" like a history of success. If you have experience working with a certain condition, then say so. Don't just say, "I can help with that." Say, "I have many clients with this challenge, and we get great results."

Remember your difference

You're likely not the only business in town offering stepping stones, and that can make it tough for clients to decide. How does someone with a digestive issue know whether to choose a nutritionist, a naturopath, a homeopath, or an herbalist (or all of them) when each one claims to have the solution to the problem? This is where the power of your difference arises. Are you an expert in this area? Does your philosophy, treatment methodology, or training give you an advantage? Remember that the person in front of you today may be in front of someone else tomorrow asking the same questions. Why should they choose you?

MEASURING SUCCESS

Stepping stones that work are worth your time. The trick, of course, is to actually *know* when they work.

To assess your stepping stones, you'll need to know if the people who sample your entry points actually become clients. For this, you'll need to track two easy numbers:

- The number of prospects (that is, the number of people who tried one of your stepping stones).
- The number of those who became clients.

That means you'll need to track how many people came to your information sessions, took you up on that free massage offer, or booked a complimentary 15-minute appointment. And you'll need to know how many of them crossed over completely and became clients.

Dividing the number of prospects who became clients by the total number of people who tried one of your stepping stones will give you your conversion rate, which is a fancy term for how well your stepping stones work. Over 80 percent of people who book a 15-minute complimentary appointment in our office become clients. Last year we did nearly 200 of these free consults. That's a lot of time—more than a week's work if you were to put them all back to back. But that "week" of work delivered a more than enough revenue to justify the investment, plus an ongoing stream of referrals and business in the years to come.

And if your stepping stone isn't working? Make it better and keep trying, or abandon it and try something else. It won't take you long to find what works. In our experience, almost everything works a little; the real goal is to find what works the *best*.

BEYOND STEPPING STONES

Right now, the vast majority of the people in your area probably aren't your customers. But that's not because there isn't a market—many people who aren't your clients likely *could* be, but the unknowns of the river are keeping them from making a leap.

To change that—to ease them across the river—stepping stones are an entry point that offers a risk-free way to resolve as many of the three "knows" as possible. A good stepping stone strategy can help your prospects safely cross the river, or at least get within jumping distance of your shore.

Information sessions, freebies, and other marketing tactics aren't new ideas. What makes the idea of stepping stones effective is *remembering their purpose*. Stepping stones aren't just about getting clients (although they do accomplish that). **Stepping stones are about getting people closer to you so they can understand how you can help.** The difference here is the *intention*. It's easy to think of stepping stones as being all about your practice, but the best stepping stones are actually about the *prospective clients*. About how you as a practitioner can make *their* lives better.

There are drawbacks to stepping stones, though.

First, they don't take away *all* of the risk of crossing the river. While they may get people closer, they don't always get them all the way across. And for some prospective clients, stepping stones don't work at *all*. For those people, the river of doubt is still too risky.

Second, and perhaps most important, many practitioners feel like their stepping stones keep them on the treadmill. After a few years of giving away freebies, attending tradeshows, or constantly seeking their next speaking opportunity, they began to feel like they spend all their time wading in the river, lugging rocks from one place to another.

When that happens, where do we turn? Do we just try harder? Add more stepping stones? Run more ads? Or do we simply give up on our stepping stones altogether?

The answer is to not to abandon stepping stones. After all, they *work*. The real solution is to understand that there's something that works *better*.

4. Bridges

Call it a clan, call it a network, call it a tribe, call it a family: Whatever you call it, whoever you are, you need one.

-Jane Howard

By the time you've finished your work, the sun has sunk low in the sky. You sit to rest your back and watch as it slowly dips toward the spine of the low hills in the distance.

At your feet, the river continues to rush past. The difference, however, is that there are now some well-placed stepping stones in the water that make it far less risky to step into the current. Placing the stones has taken some time and effort, but it's clear that they'll make the job of crossing the river much easier.

Just a few feet away, the crystal sits on a rock by the river's edge. Even in the dimming light of early evening, it shines as brightly as ever.

As you watch, its glow catches the attention of a woman on the opposite bank. Your spirits begin to soar as she looks at the stepping stones, then begins to ease her way into the current, treading carefully from stone to stone, finally reaching your side of the river. With a smile you scramble to your feet to greet her. It's your first opportunity to help since you've started the journey.

For the remainder of that day and the next, you work to help the slow trickle of people who make their way across the river for help. Occasionally someone simply wades into the river and crosses unaided, but most step from rock to rock, following the path you've created.

It's a rewarding experience, but at the same time you can't help but notice how many other people simply turn away. The light of the crystal is strong and the stepping stones are clearly visible, but many people still take one look at the river and move on.

As you ponder where you could place more stones to make the crossing easier, you notice a man standing on the opposite bank, gazing at the crystal. After a moment, he looks up at you. You smile and raise a hand in greeting, and he does the same, then steps in your direction.

But as he comes closer to the river, his smile fades as he takes in the swift, dark water. Like so many others, he shrugs ever so slightly and turns to leave.

As you watch, however, the woman you first helped the previous day passes by on the opposite bank. She greets the man with a smile. You can't hear anything over the rushing of the river, but you see the man gesture at the water several times.

And then something remarkable happens.

The woman places her hand on the man's shoulder and gently turns him to face upstream. Just at the edge of the forest, so close that you can't believe you didn't see it before, is a *bridge*. In fact, you'd swear the bridge didn't even exist just a few minutes ago.

With a broad smile, the man shakes the woman's hand and heads to the bridge. Moments later he's standing beside you. Shaking your head in wonder, you introduce yourself and get to work.

✳

When Brooke Thomas opened the doors to her Rolfing practice in Connecticut, she was on her third practice in as many states. After establishing practices in California and New York, she knew all too well how long it could take to build awareness and momentum in a new business.

Not only was Brooke in a new area and starting from scratch, but she also faced an additional challenge: she wasn't yet licensed in the state. How was she going to start to promote a practice that didn't even exist? Brooke's strategy was to build bridges.

While waiting for her licensing to be complete, she found a thriving yoga studio in her area that had a philosophy that resonated with her.

"I contacted the owners and offered free Rolfing to their teachers," Brooke recalled. "It was the best thing I ever did. They were lovely human beings, and they built my practice."

They did indeed build her practice. Brooke's strategy of connecting with other health care professionals (who could in turn connect her with clients) paid off, and as she describes it, "three months after starting a new practice in a city where I didn't know a soul, I managed to triple my income and completely fill my practice."

What happened in Brooke's practice is a practical example of finding new clients through the power of a referral—a trusted recommendation to bridge the gap between your practice and the people who might need your services.

These referrers, or "bridges," allow potential clients to cross the river safely and easily. In the real world, **bridges are trusted sources who can recommend your service without hesitation or doubt.**

When stepping stones just aren't enough, people need reassurance that what's on the other side of the river is worth the trip across. That reassurance almost always comes from someone they know and trust. A colleague. A friend or family member. Another professional.

The reassurance is what tips the scales. It's as if some of the familiarity, trust, and respect they have for the person they *do* know rubs off on the person they don't (you), and suddenly the risk just doesn't seem as great. The river becomes a non-issue because there's a bridge to guide them safely across.

Like bridges, referrals are shortcuts. They overcome the risks and objections to using your services, and they do it faster and more effectively than any other tool. Referrals are a way to deal directly with the three unknowns and bring people to your practice fully engaged and ready to become clients. Referrals can instantly create a bridge over the river and safely deliver people straight to your door—and not just as prospects, tire kickers, window shoppers, or test drivers, but as real, honest-to-goodness, paying *clients*. And unlike stepping stones (which tend to require some ongoing effort on your part), bridges take far less work in the long run and deliver far more clients. Over time, bridges are the best source of new clients for your practice.

Not all bridges are created equally, though. There are referrers who deliver many great clients to your practice, and there are those who don't. Some bridges are four-lane concrete and steel thoroughfares that allow thousands of people to pour across. Others are rickety walkways fashioned of mossy boards and vines. But they all deliver clients across the river and safely to your practice in their own way, and in varying numbers.

Just as each referral source is valuable for its own reasons, each also has its own unique characteristics. Some of those sources are close contacts like your favorite aunt, your best friend, or the chiropractor down the street. Others are your banker, your mail carrier, or your hairdresser. Some are clients who love what you do. Others are people who've *heard about* clients who love what you do.

Because each referral source is different, each needs its own unique bridge-building strategy. We're going to define three bridges to your practice and strategies for building each one so that you can choose where to direct your time and money in a way that gets the best results from each source.

BRIDGE #1: HEALTH CARE PROFESSIONALS

Let's take our bridge idea a step further. Imagine your practice is surrounded by water on all sides now—it's an island in the stream halfway between the two shores. You're going to invest in a bridge to connect you more firmly to the mainland. Your dilemma, though, is which side of the river you should build to.

To the west is the town of Wellsville. The people are vibrant, healthy, and rarely ill. They lead healthy lifestyles and are filled with energy. To the east is Illsville. For reasons no one understands, the inhabitants of Illsville are a pretty sick lot. Almost everyone has some chronic condition, and many are acutely ill on any given day.

Which town will you build a bridge to? A close look will reveal that there are far more people in Illsville who need your help. If you're going to invest time and money in a bridge, that's the place to build it to. Besides, the Wellsville people are in pretty good shape—they can use the stepping stones if they need your help.

The real-world equivalent of building that bridge to Illsville is to build referral relationships with health care professionals. They're the trusted sources who are in constant contact with the people who need your services the most.

Those referrers can be any colleague or health care-related professional such as:

- CAM practitioners like chiropractors, naturopaths, and acupuncturists.
- Conventional medical professionals such as MDs, dentists, psychiatrists, nurses, pharmacists, and other specialists.
- Other related health professionals: personal trainers, health food store staff and owners, gym employees, and others.

These folks are your colleagues—kindred professional spirits and people with related business and professional interests. Even if you don't agree with their approach, you've got a lot in common with these people and they're a potential bridge worthy of your consideration.

They also have a significant set of advantages over other referral sources. The first of these is that they tend to be *credible*. Pretend again that you've never been to a CAM practitioner.

When your Aunt Agnes tells you to see her acupuncturist, you'll most likely thank her for the advice and file it away according to what you already believe about acupuncturists. Maybe you'll go, maybe you won't. However, when that recommendation comes from a health professional whose opinion you already respect, you're more likely to act on it. The bottom line? *Professional referrals are more likely to show up at your door.* Their credentials, experience, title, and status provide a level of authority that tends to make a difference.

Not only do your professional referrers carry a big stick, but they also tend to have a lot of people to wave it at. The average busy doctor may have thousands of client files. Your Aunt Agnes, although lovely, probably doesn't have that many friends. Health professionals are often in close contact with many patients every single day, and new ones are arriving all the time. Agnes may not get out that much.

And it's not just the sheer volume of people they're in contact with. It's the fact that *all of those people are potential clients—*they all live in Illsville and can use your help. Everyone in the health professions is dealing with clients who have a health concern or health interest of some sort. It's like their clients have already been pre-selected as being in need of your help. With the exception of purchasing a practice, professional referrals provide the best source of pre-qualified clients you can find.

How to build professional referral bridges

Most health care professionals are in it for the long haul. They're building a career. If you get them to refer once, then they can refer for many years to come. Professional referrers build a very wide bridge, and for that reason it's worth both time *and* money to pursue them. The great part is that professional referrals require very little of the latter. Here are a few ways you can start to build your professional referral network:

Become a client

If you really want another practitioner to refer to you, book an appointment with her. Really—it's that simple. You can schmooze and network and lunch and send notes and letters, but nothing seems to work as well as the simple act of booking an appointment. You'll get a much better understanding of what she does, and in most cases, you'll get a decent amount of talk time in so that she can understand what you do. There's no better way to get referrals coming in from other health care professionals than to simply book some of their time.

Refer

The surest way to get is to *give*. Refer business to other professionals and they're likely to reciprocate. Once again, if you know your specialties and have a firm grasp on what you enjoy, then you can refer prospective clients who are not ideal for your particular practice to other practitioners. Not only will you be able to craft your client base around the people and problems that best suit your style, but you'll also be building your own bridges to other health professionals who may well return the favor in the future.

Intend to refer

If you're just starting out, you may not have many opportunities to refer. In that case, call other health professionals and ask if you can come by to pick up some of their cards so you can refer from your office as the need arises. You'll get a warm reception.

As with all these strategies, though, remember to maintain your integrity. If you don't have any intention of referring to a practitioner, don't waste your time pretending you might.

Ask for advice

Like most other aspects of life, asking for practice advice is a great way to get someone's ear. Almost everyone likes to be asked for his or her opinion. It's a great way to open the lines of communication with a professional who you don't know personally and to shift the nature of your relationship from being competitive to being collaborative.

Complement, don't compete

Health care professionals will be less willing to refer to you if they perceive you as being the competition. It's yet one more good reason to take the time to define your difference. You'll reduce the perception of being a competitor, and in many cases you'll be able to help other practitioners by taking the cases that they *don't* want or treating their clients in ways that clearly complement the work they're already doing.

You might be surprised to learn that your competitors can be an excellent source of new clients. But a close look will reveal that most practitioners in the same profession have some clients and conditions that they enjoy working with, and others they don't. If you can find a colleague whom you can complement, then you can both benefit from growing your practices with clients who you're likely to have success with.

We have referral relationships with colleagues within a few blocks of our office. We send clients back and forth because we understand exactly what each of us is best at. It's great for clients *and* it's great for business. Don't exclude similar practitioners from your list of potential bridges.

Get to know their gatekeepers

It can be hard to reach some busy practitioners. You may have an uphill battle trying to "do lunch" with Dr. So-And-So, but you'll always be able to reach her staff. Not only can the staff help you connect with the practitioner over time, but the staff members themselves can start referring clients your way.

Don't forget conventional care

If you wanted to find the biggest source of people needing health care anywhere, it's in the offices of conventional doctors around the world. A referral relationship with a medical doctor can do wonders for your new client numbers. Sure, they may have differing philosophies from yours, but so do most people if you dig deep enough. Before you write off your nearest MD completely, consider that physicians have some terrific advantages as referral sources.

First of all, there are *a lot* of MDs out there. As the primary health care choice for millions and millions of people, there are MDs *everywhere*. In fact, there are over 300,000 medical doctors in the United States alone. That's a lot. And those many MDs have even more clients. Millions of them. MDs are in the right market—they deal with the sick people of Illsville all day. While your client Bob may be well connected and sing your praises, not everyone he knows may need your help. Just about everyone who walks into an MD's office, however, is a potential client. Nearly all of them have a complaint of some sort.

Secondly, like other health care professionals, MDs are authority figures. The difference in our culture, though, is that they tend to carry much more clout. If Bob tells his golf buddy to see you, his buddy will think about it. If an MD tells the golf buddy the same thing, he's far more likely to go.

If you can get physicians referring to you, your practice can really take off. The challenge, however, is that the average MD can be notoriously difficult to swing to the CAM side of the fence. If you're smart about this, though, you can build a great referral network of physicians who will both refer and collaborate.

But how do you bridge the gap and develop the relationship? Here are a few MD-specific tips:

MD Tip #1: Don't take food from their plates

Or at least, don't make it obvious. Even in publicly funded health care systems, MDs can be highly territorial, so presenting yourself as competition won't help. And if you are competing directly, you don't need to brag about it. If MDs don't see you as competition, they'll be more likely to refer. This is no different from any other profession.

You'll also find your job easier if you think of yourself as being "complementary" as opposed to "alternative." This may just be semantics, but any time your clients or their doctors see things as an "either-or" choice, you're likely to lose more often than win. The key is to educate clients and doctors. Let them know that those seeking your help can see their MDs *and* you, and that the partnership is to everyone's benefit.

Conventional medicine has a strong hold on the market, and an either-or attitude makes for an uphill battle.

MD Tip #2: Make their lives easier

In most cases, you're really not selling the same thing as the average physician. Whether you're a naturopath, a chiropractor, a yoga instructor, or a traditional Chinese medicine practitioner, there's a good chance that you're exposed to a great deal of chronic or lifestyle-related complaints. These aren't the complaints that the average MD wants to field. They don't have time for them.

So sell MDs on the idea that you'll take the difficult stuff—the clients who aren't getting better or aren't generating the billing that they're looking for. Get them to refer the people who need counseling or someone to talk to. Our practice has great success with chronic and challenging issues like fibromyalgia, digestive complaints, skin conditions, and chronic fatigue—the same things that are thorns in the sides of many medical doctors. While we can help with much more, the conditions we focus on in conversation with medical doctors are those that are least enjoyable and lucrative for them to treat.

MD Tip #3: Refer

Don't hesitate to refer clients to conventional care if you feel comfortable doing so. Just like any professional, they'll appreciate it. Even if you practice in an area where MD's aren't seeking new patients, refer anyway. It sends a message that you're willing to collaborate, and appreciate the value of what they offer.

MD Tip #4: Mind the ego

Allopathic doctors are taught to be in control. To make decisions with confidence and to not second-guess themselves. It's part of their training. As such, you're likely to bump up against an ego or two.

Don't get your back up. It just doesn't matter. Respect the fact that this is how they were trained to practice and remember that many of them are not enjoying the same freedom you are. Medical doctors are frequently dealing with the painful intricacies of publicly funded health care or complicated insurance coverage. They may also be public servants, and as such they may not be as service-oriented as a private businessperson for whom every negative client interaction can cost.

The fortunate thing is that you can use an ego to your advantage. Try asking medical professionals for advice as opposed to referrals. After all, many of them run extremely busy practices and deal with rare conditions that you may have no experience with. Ask an MD for practice management advice or guidance with a particularly difficult case and you'll be surprised at how positive and productive your interactions will be.

MD Tip #5: Be professional

Nothing burns people more than having their professional opinions and status undermined. You can disagree, but you don't have to badmouth. Conduct yourself as a professional with respect to confidentiality, medical records, office procedures, and the like. Demonstrate that your standards are as high as theirs.

MD Tip #6: Be an educator

One of the barriers to referrals from other health care professionals is their perception of you and your modality. Medical professionals in particular live in an environment of increasing litigation, which is resulting in a fear of the "unknown." Add to that the fact that anyone who refers is putting her own credibility on the line, and it's easy to see why other health care professionals might *not* choose to refer to you.

For most of these professionals, their comfort level with alternative medicine is determined by their knowledge of whether the proposed treatment or modality is *effective* and *safe*. After all, medical doctors are frequently unaware of the level of training and education that many CAM practitioners receive.

The higher you can present your practice on each of these scales, the more comfortable all health professionals will be when referring to you. Look for specific evidence from established sources that support the treatments you use and put your qualifications, training, continuing education, code of conduct, and other professional indicators front and center whenever possible.

Getting personal with professionals

Brooke Thomas built her practice based on bridges to health care professionals. It was a good fit for her and it worked wonders. It will work for you, too, if you let it.

When it comes to the practicalities of connecting with professionals of all types, though, bridge building is a personal connection game. Dropping flyers to every naturopath in the yellow pages is not going to get you results. No bulk mailers, no email blasts, and no "Dear Sir/Madam" for these ones—professional referrals are a custom job. Each professional on your list needs to be approached in a systematic, personalized way.

When you do connect, make sure that you leverage each contact you make. If you meet with one professional, ask her if there's anyone else she could recommend you speak with. If she mentions names, ask if you can use her name when you contact them. Ideally, each person you contact should open at least one more door for you and provide you with more information to base your next meeting on.

You'll notice that many of these strategies for building referral bridges with other CAM professionals and with MDs are the direct opposite of *asking* someone for a referral. They're about *giving*. As Bob Burg and John David Mann note in *Go-Givers Sell More*, "The great upside-down misconception about sales is that it is an effort to *get* something from others. The truth is that sales at its best—at its most effective—is precisely the opposite: it is about giving."

Even when you're just starting out, it's not hard to find a way to give. Just remember this: it's not about *you*. Building relationships with others is about how you can help *them*. And even when you think you can't help, you can still be interested in someone else. You can always find a way to make an interaction about them, not you.

Your health care colleagues are the first bridge on our list because they're a natural starting point for practitioners who are just opening their doors. But professional referrals aren't the only bridge to help prospective clients over the river.

BRIDGE #2: YOUR EXISTING CLIENTS

While researching this book, we were amazed by how many busy practitioners never advertised. Some weren't even in the phone book. Some advertised a little at first, but gave it up altogether after a short time. Yet many were booked solid—weeks or months in advance—with a marketing budget of almost zero.

As we dug into their stories, it became clear that those practitioners had discovered perhaps the most effective secret of new client generation: **in the long run, the greatest quantity and quality of new clients for your practice will come from within.**

The longer you practice, the more you'll discover that referrals from your existing clients are perhaps the single best means of finding the clients you love the most. Professional referrals might deliver a great *quantity* of clients to your door—particularly at first—but client referrals are almost always a better fit.

Clients that fit make your life easier. They're the ones who comply with treatment, take responsibility for their health, pay their bills, and get better. Fortunately, they also tend to be the ones who refer most often. Over time, a practice filled by client referrals tends to be simpler and more enjoyable to run.

While professional referrals carry some authority, *client* referrals carry an authenticity all their own. There's no better evidence of your success as a practitioner than healthy clients. A client who's lost 40 pounds by following your advice is a walking billboard for the effectiveness of your services. A client relieved of a chronic condition billed as "unsolvable" by other professionals is a living testament to your skill. You may have an excellent brochure, advertising strategy, and website, but nothing beats the real thing, live and in person.

Not only are existing clients living proof that what you do works, but a client you've helped can be a fan for life—the best ones will become evangelists and sing your praises from the rooftops to anyone who will listen. And this type of PR is easily distinguishable from less genuine advertising testimonials. The "real thing" has a shine of its own that's very compelling.

In the long term, your practice will find the best quantity and quality of clients from within. That is the significance of the new clients in your practice. It's not the money they bring—although that's helpful. It's the bridge to others that creates a steady flow of new clients. The value of clients is not just what they can give you *now*. It's what they continue to give long after they've left your office.

How to get more client referrals

To establish our first bridge—professional referrals—we needed to build a bridge from scratch for the most part because there was no existing relationship. With your clients, however, the bridge already exists in the form of an ongoing or past relationship. You just have to open the gates and let people use it. Here are a few strategies for doing just that.

Track referrals

We've referred dozens and dozens of clients (maybe even more) to a local dentist. We've sent him literally tens of thousands of dollars of business. Do we do it because he's the best? No, although he is excellent. We do it because years ago he impressed the heck out of us with his referral tracking. His clients' files contain a dated list of other clients they've referred. Every client visit, he's able to look at the person's chart and know if she's referred anyone since her last visit.

It seems simple, but when you're sitting in his chair, it's far more magical. It's as if he's taken the initiative to personally remember the referral you sent last month and has been waiting for you to show up so he can thank you in person. It's marvelous. And as with a truly great magician, even when you know the trick you can still recommend the experience to a friend.

The lesson here is that increasing client referrals starts with tracking them. If you can't measure them, then it's hard to know where they come from. And if you don't know where clients come from, it's tough to find more of them.

This doesn't have to be complicated. You can use a system like our dentist friend does, which is entirely paper-based, or you can use a computer program. You can use a spreadsheet at the front desk or a notebook, but use *something*.

Express gratitude

Part of the problem with *not* tracking referrals is that if you can't track them, you can't *thank* the people who sent them. This is so simple that it's often overlooked. For our dentist friend, it's easy to glance discreetly in the file and say, "Thanks so much for referring Jack to us. We really appreciate it."

If you like, send a simple thank you card for the first couple of referrals. After all, these people are entrusting you with the health of their friends and family, so make sure you appreciate what that means. Some practitioners offer gifts or rewards. Do what fits you, but make sure you find a way to express your thanks.

Ask

Raza Shah, a naturopathic doctor in Ontario, has a simple strategy for gaining client referrals: he gives a business card to the "wow's."

And who are the wow's? "They're the people you *really* connect with," he said. "The ones truly blown away by what you offer." Raza knows when it happens, and so do you. They're the clients you hit a home run with, and they have the potential to become a much wider, stronger bridge to your practice. And all it takes is to simply pass them your card and say, "If you know of anyone else I can help, send them in."

What Raza is doing is so simple it's often overlooked: he's simply *asking* for referrals.

Not only do people love to be asked for help, but the act of asking makes it clear that you are indeed seeking new clients. Remember that your existing clients only see a small slice of your daily practice and may not realize you're seeking new referrals.

In our clinic, for example, we like to schedule appointments close together to maximize efficiency. We don't double-book or keep people waiting, but we try to avoid big white spaces in the appointment book. Our approach has always been that it's better to have two busy days than five days full of holes in the schedule. As a result, there's usually a modest level of traffic in the waiting room. That's great in many ways, but sometimes our busy waiting room has led people to assume that we aren't taking on new clients. We need to actively *tell* people we want more clients for them to take the final step of referring them to us.

Tell the truth

Many practitioners don't take the most fundamental step toward increasing the number of referrals coming their way—simply saying that they really would like to be busier. Many of us are uncomfortable acknowledging that our business is not as big as we'd like it to be, or we feel awkward admitting to the entrepreneurial side of our practice. "Yes, I'm always looking for more clients," is an honest and reasonable statement.

Provide exceptional service

In addition to providing great care, remember that clients need to have a *complete* experience. Are you keeping your wait times short? Are you making it easy for people to pay? Is your staff friendly, respectful, and confidential? Is your office pleasant to enter? Is parking available? Is it free? All these things add up to a complete experience that affects whether or not your clients will refer their friends. Remember that when people refer, they're putting their own reputations on the line, too.

Show your gratitude in other ways

Why not put your money where your mouth is? Throw your best referrers a freebie once in a while to show your appreciation. Include them in new office plans, testing of new protocols, and open house events. Make them feel like they're more than just another appointment in a busy CAM practice.

Help them

Above all else, if you legitimately help people resolve their health concerns, they will refer to you. If you've helped someone with a chronic condition that no one else seemed to be able to treat, you'll have earned that person's respect and referrals for years to come. Focus on providing care with integrity and passion, and the referrals will take care of themselves.

Say "I can help with that"

It's one thing to help when someone asks, but it's just as important to offer to help when they *don't*.

It's very common for clients to mention one (or both) of the following while in your care:

- Another health concern in addition to the one that brought them to you.
- A health concern of a family member or friend.

This frequently comes up as an off-hand comment or emerges as part of a case history. Instead of treating it as just additional case history data or chit chat, develop the habit of saying, "I can help with that."

And if you can't help? Then say, "I know someone who can help with that." Refer them to a trusted professional. Both your colleague and your client will be grateful for your thoughtfulness.

Teach clients when to refer

Not only do you need to say, "I can help with that," but you need to teach your clients to say it, too. Educating them on the kinds of conditions and complaints that you have great success with lets them say, "Hey—my practitioner can help with that" on your behalf.

Make it easy to refer

Remember your stepping stones? They're just as critical for your referrers as they are for your prospects. People are far more likely to refer if they can do it in a way that doesn't put their own reputations on the line. Our clients make great use of our complimentary 15-minute appointment cards because they let them refer without worrying that their friend or family member might spend their money in vain.

Include referral cards in any materials you give your existing clients. That makes it easy for your clients to give out your information, and they also get to feel like they're giving something of value to their friends, colleagues, and family members. If it's appropriate, go a step further and offer them a coupon or fee reduction that they can offer to someone. They'll get the satisfaction of helping both you *and* their friend.

BRIDGE #3: YOUR PERSONAL NETWORK

If you build solid bridges to your client base and to other health care professionals, then you'll have far more clients than ever crossing the river to join you in your practice. But clients and colleagues are only part of the collection of people who pass in and out of your life.

Personal referrals are any new clients who come to you via one of your personal contacts, such as a family member, friend, acquaintance, or non-health care business contact like your hairdresser or your lawyer. Some of these referrers may be professionals in their own right, but for our purposes, we lump anyone outside of health care into this category.

These types of referrals are particularly important during the early stages of your practice. Those leads from your friends, family members, and other personal connections are sometimes all you have coming out of the gate. And these people will often promote you vigorously because of their personal relationship with you or their gratitude for your support of their businesses in the past.

How to get more personal referrals

Talk about what you do

Don't be shy! You have an incredibly important job and there's a good chance it took a lot of hard work and sacrifice to create it. Learn to talk about what you do and to be proud of your role and your results. Don't forget, everyone loves to talk about health.

Carry cards

Simple and effective. Just keep a handful everywhere—in your wallet, purse, car, gym locker, everywhere. This strategy is simple, tried, and true. And if you use them, keep your free "meet the practitioner" cards on hand, too.

This idea isn't new. The challenge, however, is that most people don't do it because the whole idea of handing out business cards seems *icky*. That's where you need to change your thinking: This isn't about aggressively handing out cards to everyone you meet; it's simply about being able to respond to the inevitable requests for cards that you're going to receive. People really *are* going to ask for them. You don't have to do anything unethical, sleazy, or uncomfortable—just have cards with you so you can give them to people who ask. It's that easy. It's not about asking people to *take* your card. It's about people asking you if they can *have* it.

If you struggle with this, just keep some cards on hand and don't worry about the "handing them out" part. Just allow yourself, at first, to simply have them with you. You'll discover that there will be all kinds of comfortable situations where you'll be glad you have them and feel perfectly fine about handing them out.

Join a networking group

Almost every community of moderate size has some type of business networking group. Not only is this a great way to get referrals early in your practice, but it helps you to connect with other non-health care professionals whose services you may need in your practice—everyone from accountants and printers to web designers and contractors.

Some networking groups may not deliver a huge number of clients, but they're a very comfortable and friendly way to discover how easy it is to talk about what you do in a way that's easy for you and others to hear.

Join a service club

A service club like Rotary can be a great way to meet new people and get referrals. There are many different types of service clubs, and even tiny communities usually have some type of community service group. But remember that these groups usually require some actual service, too. Joining one just for the sake of extra business may not be the best thing for you or the group in question. Connecting with a group or cause you feel strongly about can be enjoyable and profitable, however, and there's nothing wrong with a win-win situation like that.

Join a church/recreation association or other interest group

Personal referrals require people. That means that just about *any* activity you're involved with is a potential source of personal referrals. Your connections don't have to come from businesses or official "networking" sources.

Book groups, gyms, walking clubs, parent groups—the list is endless, but each is an opportunity to network in a relaxed, interesting, and enjoyable way. That means more fun and more referrals.

This isn't about shoving business cards at the members of your church or in the faces of your workout partners. This is simply getting out there in a way that's rewarding to you and being proud to tell people what you do when they ask. Because they *will* most certainly ask.

Your personal network is different from other bridges. In many ways, it's far easier to work on because those contacts are already in our comfort zone. The challenge is that many of these people may not know you in your professional role or they may not be connected with people who need your services. When Brooke Thomas connected with yoga professionals she had huge success and jump started her fledgling practice from zero to full in just 30 days. But when she tried connecting with the mortgage brokers and other professionals in her building, the results were dismal. Those people shared little in common with her except their location.

The great thing about your personal network, though, is that it's *yours*. It's comfortable. It's fun. Just don't focus on it to the exclusion of the people who can create a wide bridge to Illsville or connect you to people who are truly interested in improving and preserving their health.

THE ESSENCE OF BRIDGE BUILDING

In the long run, referrals are going to be the single best source of new clients for your practice. They're inexpensive to maintain, and over time they deliver more clients than traditional marketing ever could. Add to that the fact that clients who arrive via referrals tend to be a closer fit to your ideal client, and we've got pretty compelling evidence for the long-term importance of building referral relationships.

If all this bridge building seems like a lot of effort, though, you're not completely wrong. It does take time to forge relationships. It doesn't have to be distasteful, though, and it doesn't have to be a waste of time. In fact, it can be quite the opposite. You'll meet some amazing people and learn a great deal while you're at it.

And it does get easier. The more clients you get, the easier it will be to get even more. Plus, much of your great bridge building is going to come from simply being generous, kind, and considerate. Take the time to respect people and spend a few mental moments in their shoes. Invest some energy in helping others. It's all good stuff that comes around like a karmic boomerang to deliver great stuff to your practice. In short, it's not really that hard, and most of it's fun.

The interesting thing about the strategies for attracting new client referrals is that most of them are people-based. Building bridges isn't about engineering. *It's about people.* That means that your level of referrals will reflect the level with which you actively engage with the world. It doesn't mean that you need to become a moving-and-shaking super-networker. Far from it. It *does* mean, however, that your practice success will be in part due to your ability to interact with the people around you. In the world of new clients, "reclusiveness" is synonymous with "slow growth." You don't have to be gregarious. Just get out there and *do stuff.* Engage with the world around you in your own way and you'll discover clients in places you never dreamed of.

Nutrition coach Stacey Weckstein's advice is to try as much as possible. "I was out there doing everything. Speaking, workshops, interviews," she said. "It helped me discover what works for me." Take Stacey's advice: just *try* something and begin the process of finding what works for you.

BEYOND BRIDGES: HOW TO REMOVE THE RIVER

Imagine this:

You go to bed wondering how you're going to get people across this scary, rushing river, and you wake up to find yourself fully booked by a crowd of clients who simply appeared from out of nowhere. It may sound like a fantasy, but it's very realistic. You really can fill an entire practice in a single day.

You can achieve this seemingly outrageous goal by simply purchasing someone else's practice. In fact, *buying a practice is the single fastest way there is to increase your number of new clients.* Buying a practice, particularly early on in your career, can multiply your growth overnight. You can literally go from zero to busy in one day. And the next day, this new client base of yours can start referring even more new clients to your practice.

Not only are these new clients high in number, but if you've bought the right practice, they're also a good *fit*. Who could be better suited for your alternative health care modality than someone who already uses it? When you purchase a practice, you're buying a highly targeted list of people with a very special characteristic: *they're already clients.* You don't need to convince these folks of the credibility of your profession or justify the costs of your modality. They bought in long ago.

But the story doesn't stop there. Instant growth is only part of the picture. Intensive marketing for new clients can be an enormous drain on your resources. It's easy to spend tens of thousands of dollars (and hundreds of hours of your time) on marketing when you're starting out. When you add up all the costs, and factor in how much you could be billing with that time, buying a practice starts to look a little less scary and the benefits start to look very attractive indeed.

And while it can be challenging to measure your return on money spent on marketing efforts like advertising, networking, free speaking gigs, and writing articles, buying a practice lets you measure your return very accurately. You won't have to wonder if you got your money's worth—you'll know for sure.

Nothing else can land hundreds or even thousands of clients in your lap in a single moment. Buying a practice does more than bridge the river; it eliminates it altogether.

How to buy a practice

The first barrier for most practitioners is that they don't even consider buying a practice. We regularly ask practitioners about this, and perhaps one in ten has even *thought* about it, never mind actually done it.

For most, buying a practice is a mysterious process involving accountants, lawyers, business consultants, and enormous stacks of cash. In reality, though, buying a practice is not as hard or expensive as you might think. It requires no special skills and, in many cases, doesn't require much cash.

We bought a practice by writing our own contract and exchanging a certified check for a box of client files. We're not suggesting that you *don't* get help from professionals like lawyers and accountants—just realize that buying someone else's practice is an option for everyone, even if you're not a business guru or a Wall Street mogul. You just need to *want* to. Before you do anything else, just open your mind to the idea that it's *possible*.

While every practice purchase is different, they all follow a similar process:

1. Find the practice

Once you accept that buying a practice is a good idea—and that it really *is* possible—the first step is to find someone to sell you one. You might find a practice advertised for sale, but there are many practices out there that could be for sale if you simply asked.

There are signs that someone might be motivated to sell their practice. A practitioner might be:

- Close to retirement.
- Operating more than one clinic in various geographic areas.
- Suffering financially.
- Holding other jobs or businesses as well as their practice.
- Tired, jaded, burned out, or otherwise ready for a change.

The trick, though, is that you never really know until you ask. Just like many practitioners don't consider buying a practice, most haven't thought seriously about *selling* theirs, either. **You can't know for sure unless you ask**.

You can do this personally or through an agent. If you don't want to do it yourself, ask a lawyer, accountant, or real estate agent for a referral to someone who might represent you in purchasing a business.

Making contact is often just about planting the seed. Many practitioners have never thought about selling their practices, but once they consider the idea, they may discover that it's exactly what they need.

2. Decide what the practice is worth

This is the trickiest part. There are a number of business valuation formulas and strategies, and you may need help here. Talk to your lawyer or accountant about finding someone who can help you. The amount will vary widely depending on whether you're buying client files only, real estate and equipment, or brand names, trademarks, and more. What's important, according to naturopath Raza Shah, is to remember that "When you're purchasing a practice, the person *buying* the practice is in the driver's seat. You're in control."

We used several strategies to come up with a value, but in the end our decision to go ahead with the purchase was made by asking, "How soon can we make our money back from the practice we're buying?" The answer in our case was one year, which we decided was a great return on our money. As it turns out, we had our original investment back in less than a year and the practice we purchased has continued to deliver revenue and new clients ever since.

But finding a practice for sale isn't just about a willing seller and an affordable price. It's also about finding one that's a good fit for your style of practice. Buying a practice that's radically different from what you currently have, or from how you imagine yourself practicing isn't necessarily a bad idea, but it's wise to acknowledge the differences between your styles so that you can determine whether what you're offering will speak to the client base you're considering buying.

3. Create an effective transfer plan

Effectively transferring clients from another practitioner to you starts before the deal even closes. Our contract stated, among other things, that the selling practitioner would provide a letter of introduction to all clients. Make sure you leverage the exiting practitioner's influence fully, and add those details to the contract.

For the greatest number of clients to stick with the practice, they need to know that the switch is happening, that it's good news for them, and that the selling practitioner fully endorses you. They need to get the sense that they're going to be in great hands.

4. Write and close the deal

Use a written, legal contract that includes the obligations of your transfer process. It often takes a concerted effort to get the deal signed, but keep the momentum up and stick with it.

5. Find the money

What's the single most important thing to remember when looking for the money to buy a practice? **Don't do it first.**

Don't let money hold you up. Don't abandon the idea of buying a practice because you're broke. In fact, **being broke is the best reason there is to buy a practice**.

This is a stretch for some people to grasp, but we do it in other areas of our life all the time. Many of us, for example, need a car to get to work, so we make the investment because it delivers a return—it lets us show up and get paid. If your practice is currently suffering, or if you're just starting out, an infusion of new clients can do the same thing: help you get paid. If you've done your homework, buying a practice can turn around your finances overnight and easily justify the investment.

And as for the money, there are a number of options. You can borrow it from a bank—after all, a practice is an asset and it has value. If you can't get a loan, you may be able to borrow money privately. Or you can convince the person selling the practice to finance the deal. In that scenario, you might pay the previous owner a monthly payment for the practice (with reasonable interest attached) instead of all the money up front. Or pay them just for the patients who transfer to your care. The options are endless. Just don't be put off because you don't have a stack of cash in your mattress to buy a practice. You don't need it.

The two biggest things stopping most practitioners from purchasing a practice and making a huge leap in their growth are that they don't think it's worth it, and that they don't think they *can*. Nothing could be further from the truth. As long as you get help and act wisely, buying a practice is a *great* investment. And anyone can do it. You don't need any special talents—there are plenty of skilled people out there who can help.

Bridges take time, and it's easy to be distracted by other marketing efforts that seem to deliver quicker results. You might feel like you should focus all your efforts on stepping stones, for example, because they tend to deliver clients *now*, while bridges take longer to pay off.

But bridges take time and energy to build because they're profoundly important. They're an investment in your future practice. Each referral relationship you build delivers an ongoing stream of clients to your door, with less and less effort over time. Imagine your practice a few short years from now. Do you want to be chained to the marketing wheel, spending thousands of dollars and untold hours promoting your practice, or would you like to rise above that?

Next to your actual clients themselves, referral relationships are the most valuable things you can create in your practice. Be sure to give them the time and energy they deserve.

RECOGNIZING THE RIVER IN PRACTICE

Almost every profession has its river. There will always be people who are uncertain about what you offer. It's normal. The river will always be there. What you need to know is how to recognize when the river is stopping you from moving further along the path to Success.

In many ways, identifying the river in your practice is easier than identifying the cave. Where the cave can be an intangible challenge, there are obvious signs that the waters of the river are high and keeping prospective clients. These signs include:

- Not having enough new clients.
- Spending more and more money on advertising without getting better results.
- Expecting people to simply "sign up" without asking questions or understanding how you can help.
- Being reluctant to offer *any* of your time without compensation, particularly early in practice.
- Being frustrated with skeptics or people who don't immediately grasp what you do after hearing your professional title.
- Attracting a great deal of prospects to your practice but failing to convert them into paying *clients*.
- Spending much of your time growing your practice without actually engaging with the world (such as by overusing the internet and other tools that keep you at arm's length from people).

The river is what separates you from your prospective clients. Its currents and chilly water represent the barriers that prevent people from becoming customers—everything from time and money to fear and apathy. Finding ways to get people across the river—from stepping stone marketing efforts that bring people closer, to referrers who bridge the river by sending clients directly—is a fundamental challenge faced by all practitioners.

As we're about to discover, though, it's not the last challenge on the journey to Success.

It's time to head back to the path.

INSIGHTS FROM THE RIVER

The river is the barrier between you and the people who aren't yet your clients. It represents the risks that potential clients perceive—like cost, credibility, time and effectiveness—that keep them from joining your practice.

Advertising only gets people to the water's edge. To get them across, you'll need:

STEPPING STONES

Risk-free ways for prospective clients to get to know you and understand how you can help.

BRIDGES

Relationships with trusted sources who can recommend your services without hesitation.

PART III: THE BOULDER

Making the Most of Your Client Base

If you can find a path with no obstacles, it probably doesn't lead anywhere.

-Frank Howard Clark

*B*ack on the path, you've covered considerable ground. Your journey has become easier with each passing day. More and more people are crossing the river on the stepping stones and bridges you've created along the way, and you realize that you're no longer alone on the journey. You're helping every day, and with each person who joins you on the path for part of the journey, you feel yourself drawing closer to Success. You're making progress.

One afternoon the path narrows from a wide track to a thin footpath, and before long you find yourself walking carefully between a cliff wall on your left and a sheer drop to the river below on your right. It's not particularly dangerous but it slows your pace. All that changes, though, when you round the next corner.

You stop short as you come face to face with an enormous boulder. It's huge and spans the entire path. With the cliff wall on one side and the river on the other, you can't go around it. What's worse is that no amount of shoving seems to budge the rock an inch. Even when you decide to retrace your steps a little and climb a tree for a better look, you get nothing more than a peek at some hills in the distance. There's no sign of another route.

Undaunted, you decide to stop for the day. After all, there are now a number of people who need your help. There's work to be done.

But the next morning, of course, the boulder is still there. Determined to move ahead, you put your shoulder against the rock and push with every ounce of strength. Nothing.

The next day brings more of the same.

You're becoming frustrated. The note said, *follow the path to its end*, yet the path is clearly blocked. Day after day you put your shoulder against the rock, and although it occasionally moves a little, most of the time you end up exhausted and no better off than before.

As the days pass you realize that although the bridges and stepping stones behind you are bringing people to you, you're not drawing any closer to Success yourself.

One day, after another herculean effort to shift the boulder leaves you sore and no further ahead, you slump to the ground, exhausted. You feel as if Success would be within your grasp if you could just get past this barrier, but it's no use. You just can't do it.

Karen is a holistic practitioner with knack for marketing. She's active in just about everything, it seems. Clubs, service groups, volunteer organizations—she's a member of many. She does a great job of inviting the media to events and notifying the public of the goings-on in her holistic practice.

She recently moved her practice from a drab office building to a new street-front location and the visibility has paid off. Despite the increased rent, the exposure is delivering new clients regularly. She collects testimonials, runs contests to attract new faces, and has a great gratitude policy in place to thank her clients for referring new people to the clinic.

Last year she expanded her advertising into more newspapers, magazines, and directories. She had a website set up and began to dabble in social media to help spread the word even farther. She runs workshops, brings in well-known guest speakers, and is in charge of several major sporting events that expose thousands of additional people to her clinic each year. Her community involvement has also connected her with dozens of great referrers who now send her a steady supply of new clients.

Karen, in short, sees *a lot* of new clients. So many, in fact, that she's been able to hire more practitioners to help her.

Despite this steady supply of new customers, however, Karen admitted that she was feeling frustrated. "It's like I'm on a treadmill," she confessed. "I have all these clients, but I'm constantly looking for more of them."

Karen had left the cave behind early in her practice. She knows what she has to offer, to whom, and how to reach those people. She's invested in herself to fill the gaps in her education about the business side of practice, and it's paid off handsomely. And along the way she's learned through trial and error the best ways to get clients to the river's edge and guide them across on stepping stones and bridges.

But now she's facing something new. After a few years in practice, Karen is beginning to feel like she isn't getting anywhere. Although she doesn't know it, Karen is facing the boulder—a common obstacle to moving closer to that mysterious Shangri-La of private practice known as Success.

The boulder is the third challenge in practice and one that we all face at some point. Just as you think you've mastered the art of marketing your practice and attracting new clients, you begin to feel like you're still not getting anywhere. It's as if you show up each day, you work, and you go home. Then you get up and do it all over again.

The boulder is that sense of spinning your wheels in practice. That feeling that even though you're constantly attracting more clients and exposing what you offer to a wider audience, you still can't quite make ends meet. You keep getting better at what you do, but you feel like your entire existence is wrapped up in looking for new clients and there's no end in sight. You wonder if the rest of your life is going to be consumed by writing articles and online content, networking, booking speaking gigs, running information sessions and creating new marketing materials.

Unable to move the boulder, many practitioners do exactly what Karen did: resolve to work even harder at getting more new clients. They market diligently. They build more bridges. They advertise like mad and create new stepping stones. When new faces show up, they treat them and get right back out there and market some more. Then they repeat the process.

Despite all the effort, though, the schedule doesn't seem to fill up the way it should. Regardless of all the new clients, there never seems to be enough cash in the bank at the end of the month to justify your hard work.

When we met with Karen, we asked her, "What is it that makes your clients come back to you over and over again?"

Her answer summed up the challenge of the boulder perfectly: "They don't."

Karen's practice is based on acutely treating new clients for a single issue, then sending them on their way. The storage area of her practice is filled with boxes of old client files. Most of her former clients have never been seen or heard from since their initial complaint was resolved.

What was happening figuratively was that new people kept crossing the river on bridges and stepping stones to see Karen, but *she wasn't taking them any farther along the path.* Remember—the practitioner's journey is a *shared* journey, and your clients need to find their way to Success, too.

What was happening *literally* was that Karen wasn't making the most of her clients.

Finding new clients—particularly early in practice—can be time consuming and expensive. If you attract them to your practice but they never come back again, then it really does feel like there's something blocking your progress. **The challenge of the boulder is that you can't reach Success without leveraging your client base.** With the boulder blocking the way, you might greet them and have some initial time together, but because no one can get past the boulder, the clients wander about and eventually head back to the other side of the river.

A practice that only sees new clients is a hard practice to build. But to make matters worse, other practitioners you know appear to be moving boulders around like titans. They seem to shove rocks out of the way effortlessly and move on even more quickly toward Success. How do they do it?

The answer is that they know more about Greek history than you do.

Archimedes, the famous Greek scientist, mathematician, and all-around smarty-pants, is best known for his "eureka" moment. During a bath he realized that he could determine the volume of an object by the amount of water it displaced. But Archimedes is also known for the first serious written explanation of the *lever*— an object that can be used to multiply the force applied to another object.

When you played on a seesaw as a kid, you were using a lever—you just didn't know it. If you think back to your seesaw days, you might remember that the seesaw worked best when you and your friend were about the same weight. If your friend was too heavy, you spent most of your time dangling in the air, kicking your legs like crazy and trying to get your end to come back down. It was a pretty powerless feeling, being stranded way up there.

It's not so different from the way we feel in practice when we face the boulder. We feel so small, and the boulder seems so big, that it's as if we could never hope to move it.

But think back to the seesaw. If you experimented a little, you might have discovered that if you moved farther out on the seesaw—so you were just about falling off the end of it—then you could get your end to come back down. You could, in effect, apply a great deal of force with just your small weight by changing where you pushed on your seesaw lever.

What you were doing by shifting yourself around was effectively changing the *length* of the lever. That created the same effect as weighing more—or *pushing harder*. What also worked was having a second friend climb onto your end of the seesaw with you. That let you push even harder still on the lever and shift your heavier friend into the air.

Archimedes once said about levers, "Give me a place to stand on, and I will move the earth." Of course, he said it in Greek, but his point was this: levers are powerful tools. We may not shift the whole earth, but we're going to pay homage to Archimedes not only because anyone who does his best thinking in the bathtub is okay by us, but also because the idea of the lever applies directly to your practice. It's a tool for doing more with less, for taking your strengths and multiplying them for better effect. The same principles that allowed you to do more with less on the playground can be applied to your practice as well.

Let's go back to the seesaw. Imagine that instead of having your heavy friend sitting on the other end, you've got it tucked under that boulder blocking the way to Success. Your seesaw is a lever, and we're going to use it to shift that big rock.

We know from Archimedes that the longer the lever, the more force we'll be applying when we push. A longer lever, then, is going to let us do more with less effort. Stand close to the rock and push and we might barely see the rock shift. But use a longer lever and, with the same effort, we can move it a great deal. The further you move along the lever—in effect, the *longer* you make the lever—the *more* you'll be able to move the rock. And the more you can move the rock, the more wealth, balance, joy, and success you can reach on the other side.

Since we're not going to bring a seesaw into your practice and start waving it around, we need to identify its real-world equivalent. The question at this point, then, is *what are the literal equivalents of the different levers?* What are the leverage points in practice to shift the boulder and allow us to continue on to Success?

The answer is that your *clients* are the leverage points. You're not going to move that boulder alone. You need *them* to climb onto the seesaw with you to make the difference.

The next three chapters look at three different "levers" for moving the boulder. They can all be used by practitioners in solo practices—they don't require you to find an associate, rent space to another practitioner, or hire someone. Each one leverages your client base a little more so that you can do more with less effort, gradually shifting the rock and clearing the road ahead.

5. The First Lever

An ounce of loyalty is worth a pound of cleverness.

-Elbert Hubbard

*T*here is a natural progression to starting a practice. After opening your doors, the first order of business is, of course, to get as many new clients as possible, as quickly as possible. Thus far on the journey, we've been focused on discovering how to define what you offer to whom and how to find those people and attract them to your practice.

Unfortunately, a natural second step in the journey for many practitioners is to forget all about these clients once they leave the office. As in Karen's practice, the file goes safely into the cabinet (or if there are no files, the name just vanishes into the ether or inside a shoebox for bookkeeping at a later date), and the next time it comes out is when the client takes the initiative to call for an appointment. That's a recipe for spending the rest of your practice career struggling for more and more new clients to replace the ones who get better, move, die, or simply drift away. It's not a pretty sight and it doesn't shift the boulder even an inch.

Fortunately there's a solution. Welcome to the first lever—the first position on our figurative seesaw that's going to help shift the Success-blocking boulder by helping you get more from the clients you already have.

The first lever is *more return visits*. This is where you start to reap the rewards of the work and expense you invested in attracting new clients from across the river to your practice. In this chapter, we'll begin to turn our focus from the external world of prospects and new clients to the internal world of the existing clients in your practice.

The simple truth of the first lever is this: **clients who come back can help move the boulder.** They can help *push*, figuratively speaking, by climbing on the seesaw and adding their weight to yours. So, the first lever is about asking, "How do I get my clients to come back more often?"

Why? First of all, new clients are expensive and getting them can be a lot of work. In fact, if you were to add up the time and money you spend marketing, educating, and networking to attract new clients and referrers, you might be shocked to discover how lucrative new clients are *not*. Fortunately, new clients can make themselves worthwhile in the long run, if they come back. Over time they require less investment and become more profitable. Once you attract a new client, you want to make sure you make the most of your investment.

Second, from a client perspective, one visit is often not enough to cure what ails. Wellness takes both time and the close relationship that comes from multiple visits.

What's most important to remember is that *you can't move the boulder alone*. Building a successful business requires new clients, but it also requires them to *return*. If you turn to ask for help shifting the boulder only to find that everyone's gone back to the other side of the river and forgotten about you, you'll never move any farther down the path.

The more often your clients come back for your help, the more often they can offer theirs.

Why Clients Come Back

You'd think that once a client knows his way across the river, coming *back* wouldn't be such a big deal. The risk is low and the level of familiarity high; there's just not that same sense of the unknown that people face before they become clients.

As it turns out, though, that's not the case. Left to their own devices, clients are notorious for doing just the opposite. **Even when they want to come back, many clients just don't.**

Unless, of course, you do something about it.

This isn't about trying to convince people to continue to do something that isn't helpful. It's not about unnecessary treatments or repetitive visits for no reason. Far from it. This is about ensuring that no one stands in the way of the best care for your client—including your client herself.

Sure, there will be people who don't (and probably shouldn't) return to your practice. Perhaps you can't help or it's not a fit for them. But there are plenty of people who could, should, and *want* to return to your practice, but don't. Maybe they're busy. Short of cash. Forgetful. Sick (ironic, yes, but it happens).

Those people can help move the boulder. But how can we get them through the doors again?

Clients return regularly to your practice for five reasons. Address these reasons and you'll find a regular supply of familiar faces to help shift the boulder and clear the route to Success.

Reason to return #1: There's a plan

During a recent visit to our office, a client commented that another practitioner she'd been seeing had told her to return in three months. When asked how the follow-up visit went, she commented, "I never went. They never told me *why* I should go."

Most of us have a reasonable handle on the short term. We can safely deal with a series of visits for an acute issue. But it's astonishing how many practitioners never give their clients any reason whatsoever to return in the long run. New clients come, new clients leave, and it's assumed they'll just come back. That's a big assumption, though. It assumes that they understand *why* and *when* they should come back. It also assumes they're going to come back to *you* and not to someone else.

So why don't we just provide the *why*? At the core, many practitioners don't give their clients a clear reason to come back because *they don't know what it is themselves.*

The first step in getting clients to return is for you to clearly understand when and why they should return.

Perhaps one of the best examples of an industry that's been successful in this process is dentistry. At one time a dentist was someone you went to when you had a problem. Sore tooth? Cavity? Injury? See your dentist.

Over time, however, your dentist evolved from someone you saw when you had a problem to someone you saw to *prevent* a problem. Want to *avoid* that sore tooth? See your dentist.

And now? Your dentist is also a beauty specialist, straightening, cleaning, and whitening your smile. So you can visit your dentist's office even more often because they keep you *looking* good.

Let's look at what this shift has meant to dental clients first. Instead of coming in response to a problem (like a toothache), clients now come for regular preventive visits. The result for the client? Fewer cavities, less pain, better teeth.

And what about the dentist? She now has increased and *predictable* cash flow. A new client now means not just the occasional emergency visit (and who can predict when those might occur?), but also a lifetime of semi-annual visits.

So how do we become more like the dentist (without, you know, actually *being* one)? The answer is to build a health care *model*—a philosophy of long-term care that benefits your clients and, as a result, you.

To discover a model that's best for your practice *and* the health of your clients, you'll need to answer the following questions. As you answer them, forget about the financial cost to the client. Think only of the health benefits.

- Would making regular visits to your office be of benefit over the entire lifespan of any client in your practice?

- Why? Generate at least five benefits from regular visits. (No, really. Do it. Stop and at least mentally generate them. Better yet, write them down.)
- How frequently would a client have to come to gain those benefits?
- What would you do at those visits?

What you're building here is a model for long-term health maintenance (or "disease prevention," or "wellness"—you can describe it in the way that best fits you). This is a return visit protocol that is independent of acute conditions, illness, and injuries. It's a protocol for *long-term* health.

Protocols help you clearly map the road to health for your clients, and the better you map it, the more readily and fully they'll follow the route. And they work for both and short and long-term health care.

Let's say your client wants to quit smoking. Which is going to be more appealing, enduring, and understandable for them—a series of follow-up appointments with no clear end, or a "Quit Smoking Program" that involves seven separate visits using treatment tools X, Y, and Z? Protocols clarify the path forward for clients. And contrary to popular belief, they don't remove your ability to treat your clients as individuals—protocols actually *enhance* it by giving you the framework for telling your clients when and why to return for more care.

Can you have more than one protocol? Certainly. It's only natural that you might require different return visit protocols for the elderly, for young children, and for people with chronic or congenital conditions. What's important is that *every client in your practice should have a long-term health protocol that involves regular visits*. It's good for their health, and it's good for your practice.

Reason to return #2: You tell them to

When we asked her how she gets her clients to come back, Heather Furby of Body Logic simply said, "I ask them." Yes, sometimes it really is that simple.

Heather's simple answer is the doorway to the biggest secret of practitioners whose clients return regularly:

Clients come back because you tell them to.

That's it. Not because you suggest, recommend, hope, argue, plead, or persuade, but because you are the professional and they expect you to tell them what to do. After all, that's why they came to see you in the first place. You're the expert. The *authority*.

Let's clarify: becoming comfortable as an authority in the client-doctor relationship doesn't mean becoming *authoritarian*. It means recognizing that you are an expert in your area of focus. You've studied it, practiced it, and presumably had some success at it. Don't be afraid to tell your client when you need to see them next. If your health care model calls for regular return visits, then explain the importance of them. And then, as an authority in your field, *tell* them when to come back.

This principle is at work all around us. We change the oil in our vehicles after a prescribed number of miles. We change the batteries in our fire alarms or smoke detectors at regular dates. We don't do these things because *we* know the subtleties of engines or batteries, we do it because someone *told* us.

Tell your clients to come back. Confidently say, "This is when I need to see you next." If you need to see them once a year, or twice a year, or 12 times a year, tell them that and then teach them *why*.

Reason to return #3: It's worth it

Not only do your clients need to know when and why to come back, but they also need to experience the *value* in coming back to see you.

Value isn't the same as price. When you shop for groceries, for example, you buy tomatoes at a certain price. But the value isn't the price alone. It's the *price per pound*. You might decide that the price per pound is a deal for tomatoes, or you might decide it's too expensive, but in either case, you're making your decision based on value.

Value is the benefit per dollar. For your tomatoes, it's the benefit you get (a pound of tomatoes) divided by the price you pay. More benefit for a lower price means more value. And the more value you get from a store, the more likely you are to shop there again.

Health care, though, is more complicated than tomatoes. In health care, people still pay in dollars, but the benefit part of the equation gets tougher to measure. Everyone has a unique idea of what a "benefit" is. For one client, it's symptomatic relief. For another, it's a cure. For someone else, it's great service, an understanding ear, or an unhurried visit with someone who can truly take the time to explain how the body works.

As health care providers, it's tough to know what's going to trigger each client's benefit button—but we can make a pretty good guess. Here are a few strategies that help clients see the benefits more clearly:

Measure things

Tomatoes are easy because we measure by the *pound*. Health is harder to measure. The skin rash subsides a bit, the pain dulls, the symptoms wane—but by how much? To make things more challenging, healing can happen so slowly at times that your clients may not appreciate that you helped *at all*.

Clients need to know that their hard work, time, and money are getting them somewhere. They need to know you're helping. They need to see road markers during their trip that indicate progress, and the best tools for the job are objective measures.

There are assessment tools for every aspect of health. In addition to standard physiological health measures like heart rate, blood pressure, body composition, and weight, there are objective measures for even the most subjective constructs like "happiness." Each measure can provide a benchmark for demonstrating how far a client has come from when they first stepped through your door. There are lab tests, online assessments, paper questionnaires, and more. There is something for every practitioner, ranging from simple and subjective to scientific and complex.

Find something you can measure, and you'll find your clients returning far more often.

Help them feel better

In the end, there will be no greater testament to your value as a practitioner than the health of your clients.

In our clinic, our guiding principle is very simple: to help people feel better. We've chosen those words carefully, though, because success in health care doesn't always mean *cure*.

Sometimes people don't get better. Sometimes they get worse. Sometimes they get *much* worse. But regardless of what happens, we can always strive to help people feel better for having been to our office. We can support them, refer them, educate them and treat them with respect. These are all things that make a client's trip to your office worth it. In other words, we might not have the reddest, the ripest or the cheapest tomatoes this week, but we can still offer them in an environment that encourages people to come back.

Your clients need simple success markers besides "cure." They need to understand that their first success might be simply being able to bend over to reach their shoes, to sleep for longer than two hours at a stretch, or to eat one vegetable.

If you want your clients to see the value in what you offer, make sure you clearly define realistic success benchmarks that they can understand, and create an environment where *every* visit is a success in some way. The more success, the greater the benefit, and the more often your clients will return.

Don't overload

It may seem like the best way to tweak the value equation in your favor is to simply offer *lots*. To give more tomatoes, so to speak. But that's not always true.

Here's a scenario: A new practitioner opens her doors. She's fresh out of school and a little freaked out by how much she's decided to charge clients. *I hope people aren't turned off by the price,* she thinks.

Anxious to make sure she's "worth it" to her clients, her first client visits are blockbusters. Lots of face time and tons of handouts, meal plans, research studies, and recipes—a veritable rainforest of paper. Satisfied that she's over-delivered, she sits back and waits for the return visit.

Sadly, it never comes.

Why? The problem is twofold. The first is that clients don't *want* the information overload. A recent survey of patients of natural medicine listed "too much information" as one of the top things that they liked *least* about their visits. People are overwhelmed as it is, and more information is not what they need. *Information overload does not help clients.* Taking a complex and extraordinarily difficult process like lifestyle change, for example, and trying to provide it all in one visit is not only impossible, but it's also overwhelming and discouraging. Like tomatoes, there's only so much information a client can digest in one sitting.

The second problem is that if you give them all the information, clients feel like they don't *need* to come back. They decide that information—not support, coaching, or insight—is all they need, and they opt to save their money and go it alone, often unsuccessfully.

The solution is to take baby steps. Resist the temptation to tell your clients *everything*, or to try to solve all their problems on the first visit. Stretch it out in manageable steps, and *tell* them that you're going to stretch it out in manageable steps. And when you're tempted to hand out that stack of paper, or treat seven different problems at once, ask yourself, *Am I really helping?* Is your client capable of making huge, all-encompassing life changes, or are you scaring her off? Would focusing on one problem this time move her closer to health?

Sometimes, one really fantastic tomato offers more value than a whole bag of mediocre ones.

Do something

Many CAM therapies involve clients carrying the bulk of the workload. Quitting smoking, exercising, eating better, dealing with life stresses and emotional issues—these are all treatments in which the client often does the actual "work." Naturopaths, nutritionists, and practitioners involved in the counseling side of alternative health often rely heavily on this type of "client-driven" treatment.

Other professions like chiropractic, massage, and acupuncture involve the practitioner "doing things" to the client—inserting needles, making adjustments, manipulating tissues. They're called "practitioner-driven" treatments.

If you're in a profession where the client does the work, then take this to heart: *clients love having things done "to" them.* If you tell people they need to exercise or change their diet, they might never come back. But if you help them become more active, measure something *and* give them supplements, they'll shout from the rooftops and book their next visit.

If you rely solely on lifestyle change with your clients, you may want to look for more practitioner-driven treatments to add to the equation. When you do, you're changing the value equation again: you're increasing the perceived benefit so that the value seems higher.

Even though client-driven changes can be essential to real long-term health, the sad truth is that many people really don't want to eat better and be more active. They want you to give them a magic bullet and charge them for it. Prescriptive health care is popular because it's easy. It may not be the end solution for your clients, but adding a practitioner-driven component to your practice helps engage clients *and* buys you the extra time you need to help coach them through the tougher changes on their own.

Reason to return #4: You're on their radar

By many measures, Alexandra Jamieson has made her mark. The author of *The Great American Detox Diet* and *Living Vegan for Dummies*, she has also been featured on Oprah and in the Oscar-nominated hit movie, *Super Size Me*.

A certified health and nutrition counselor, Alex works with individuals and groups to help people discover the power of healthy eating and detoxification. Not surprisingly, given her background, she's a busy practitioner. When we asked her what the secret to her success was, though, her response was as surprising as it was simple: "Building an email list over time. Being consistent and sending out a newsletter consistently that speaks to my core audience."

While being on Oprah and in a blockbuster documentary can't hurt, remember that those things don't shift the boulder. They only help bridge the river. It's staying in touch with clients that keeps you top of mind and ensures that they remember to continue to pursue health—and to do it with *you*.

Fortunately, we live in an age where staying in touch is easier than ever. You can create newsletters, email promotions, blogs, and print mailings with ease. Just find a way to stay in touch with your clients that works for you and stick with it.

Yes, your regular marketing for new clients also helps keep you top of mind with existing ones, but developing material specifically for your clientele creates a sense that they are "something special." When you treat the people who've crossed the river differently from the ones who haven't, you create greater loyalty.

We send out regular print and email newsletters to our client base. It takes very little time, and even the print mailings, which cost considerably more, always more than pay for themselves with repeat visits and reactivated clients. Rolfer Brooke Thomas uses a more personal approach, writing to clients individually as she thinks of them. "Warm, individual correspondence is a dying art," she says. "As a result, it gets noticed."

Regardless of your approach, make a point of building an up-to-date client database, including email addresses. It allows you to stay in touch with minimal effort. For some practitioner-friendly tools to help you do this, visit practitionersjourney.com.

Reason to return #5: Good processes

Even practitioners who have all the ingredients for return visits—exceptional models for long-term care, great success, authority, and more—often stumble because they lack the simple systems in their practice to make sure all this theory translates into the reality of clients actually showing up.

Here's a simple (but common) scenario. You tell your client, "Let's book you in again in two weeks so we can check your progress," or some variation that would happen in your practice. But when you open the calendar to schedule the appointment, the client says, "I'll have to call you. I'm not sure when I'll be back from my business trip."

You and your client part ways and you go back to the details of practice. And in many cases, life "happens" and your client never quite makes it back.

Clients "falling through the cracks" (getting lost or forgotten in the details of day-to-day practice) make it that much harder to shift the boulder. There are a number of reasons why this can happen:

- Your client is unsure about her schedule (as above) and needs to "check" and get back to you.
- You're waiting for further information to proceed—lab testing, nutritional diaries or other client homework, imaging, files from other practitioners, et cetera.
- Your client needs to wait for another pay cycle, or for insurance, or for other financial issues that cause them to delay the next step in care.

When this happens, there's a tendency to just wait for the client to call when they have the money, the time, the information, the energy, or whatever else it is that's holding up the process. But when we wait, two things happen: we lose control of the process, and we begin to *forget*. You can't rely on your memory or your client's initiative for return visits. You need to have a process in place.

In our office, if we can't get the client to commit to a next step (and it's reasonable that they might not want to), we enter a reminder into our system for a date in the future and we call them. We use software to remind us, but we could just as easily use a paper calendar. It's a simple system that does one thing well: it reminds us to remind *them*.

You can build whatever process you want that works for you. It doesn't matter if you have a physical office or work online. You might have a paper appointment book or scheduling software. You might be a Rolfer or a reiki practitioner, a nutritionist or a naturopath. All of these factors will contribute to a unique process that works for your practice. But regardless of those details, your process has to conform to two rules:

- Every patient leaves the office knowing when they need to come back (because there's a plan, as we saw in Reason #1).
- You never, ever rely solely on the client to contact *you*. You can let them call, but you need a backup system so they don't fall through the cracks.

In a new practice it's easy to get into the habit of relying on your memory. Get out of that habit. The day will come (if it hasn't already) when memory just isn't enough.

BEYOND THE FIRST LEVER

Clients never stay on your side of the river *forever*. Their lives are elsewhere. After some time with you, they need to cross back over and return to their families, their jobs, and their homes.

But if you follow the strategies of the first lever, you'll notice that there are a lot more people on your side of the river a lot more often. That means you'll always be able to find someone to help climb on that seesaw lever and shift the boulder just a fraction further. It means you won't be *alone*. Every client visit is an extra shoulder against the boulder, and every bit counts.

The first lever is about moving the boulder by having more people pushing on it more often. But what if the boulder isn't moving *enough?* The good news is that there's more leverage available to us. If you want to move the boulder farther and faster with the clients you have, then you'll need to add something else to the equation.

6. The Second Lever

"Life is pretty simple: You do some stuff. Most fails. Some works. You do more of what works. If it works big, others quickly copy it. Then you do something else. The trick is the doing something else."

-Tom Peters

*J*osh is a talented TCM practitioner who's been in business for nearly a decade. He set up shop in his hometown, so he got off to a strong start in new client growth. His family name was well known and referrals came fairly readily as he was the only practitioner in his local area.

With a head start on the journey under his belt, Josh carefully nurtured each client—putting the first lever to work by ensuring that they stayed engaged in his practice and returned to his office when warranted.

As a result, Josh has become a very busy guy. In fact, his practice is booked solid with a waiting list. But while things are good, Josh has a sense that they could be better.

Josh, like many practitioners, would like to increase his income. He has a new child and knows he should start saving more for the future. The challenge for Josh, though, is that he'd also like to stay sane. Work-life balance is important, and Josh feels he's already at his limit. The only way he can make more money is to work more hours, and for him, that's not a sustainable solution. Working more is a shortcut around the boulder that eventually leads not to Success, but to Burnout.

Josh is pushing against the boulder. And he's got some help from his clients, too. But it's still not moving as far or as fast as he'd like. He's got Success in his sights, but he can't seem to get there. He still feels stuck.

If you're like Josh, you're out of time, out of room, and possibly out of money, too. Where do you head next? You already have your clients showing up regularly to help push on the boulder, but you can't quite move it enough to slip past.

But what if they all pushed a little *harder?*

Welcome to the second lever. It's time to look at a way to move the boulder a little farther and a little faster with each push—to get more of the leverage that Archimedes described. And the best part is that even if you're not as busy as Josh, it's never too early to start. This works whether you have ten clients or a thousand.

THE SECOND LEVER: MORE REVENUE PER VISIT

The real-world equivalent of pushing "harder" on the boulder is for your clients to *spend* more in your practice each time they visit. In other words, for you to generate more revenue from the same number of client visits. The second lever is about asking yourself, "How can I increase the revenue of my practice without increasing the number of clients or client visits?"

Let's start by being specific in business terms about what we're trying to do. Our objective with the second lever is to increase your *average revenue per visit.* That's your annual practice revenue divided by the number of client visits.

For example, if your practice billed a total of $82,000 last year, and you had 1,600 client visits, then your average revenue per visit was 82,000/1,600, or $51.25 per visit. Your numbers may be much higher, or much lower, but the formula is the same no matter how busy you are.

What if we found a way to add $20 on average to a client visit? Then for our example, the average revenue per visit would become $71.25. What's the big deal about an extra $20? Well, that increased average would make the *same practice*, with the *same clients* and the *same amount of your time*, generate $114,000 in a year.

Let's be clear about this: the *exact same practice* would generate an extra $32,000 with no extra client visits.

How is this accomplished? There are three key strategies for increasing your revenue per client with the second lever:

1. Raise your rates
2. Add products or services
3. Bundle products and services

Strategy #1. Raise your rates

Perhaps the easiest way to raise your overall practice income without adding a single client is to raise your prices. Despite the seeming simplicity of this, however, it's often either overlooked or avoided.

A lot of the reason for this lies in our discomfort with our current rates. We're often reluctant to raise prices that we already feel uneasy about. To get past that, we need a compelling reason. Here are a few:

Inflation

Prices rise over time—or, conversely, your dollars buy less over time. Just ask your parents (or anyone significantly older than you) what they got paid at their first job and you'll hear about how little per hour they made, how a movie cost a nickel, and how kids these days don't appreciate... okay, you get the point. We've all heard it. But the message is sound: the world gets more expensive as time goes by, and most practitioners ignore this shift. Every year, the cost of running your business and your life increases. The rent, equipment, services and supplies your practice uses creep upward in price. Sometimes that creep is very slow—almost imperceptible—but it's there. If you go for five years without raising your rates, you'll be taking home less money.

Raising your prices is something you should consider periodically. It's got nothing to do with overcharging or being elitist or pricing yourself out of the market—it's simply keeping you in business. Imagine if you were running that movie theater today and still charging a nickel admission and three cents for popcorn.

Like the movie theater owner, you'll eventually struggle if your rates never change.

You're better than you were last year

It's true. You now have more experience and your skills have improved. (If you've gotten worse since last year, then pricing is *not* your number one problem.) You are gradually becoming an expert in your chosen field of alternative medicine and your clients are reaping the benefits. Over time, that expertise is worth more in the marketplace. Why should a shiny new practitioner make the same as you, the 15-year veteran?

More profit

We're not suggesting that you be greedy, but remember that when you raise your rates by five percent, you've pretty much added that extra cash to your pre-tax income. There are no extra expenses associated with the rate increase. It is, essentially, extra money.

"What if I lose clients?" you might ask. It can happen, but you may find that a price hike lets you keep your best customers and make more profit on fewer total clients. That, in turn, translates into better work-life balance. You may also find that nothing at all changes—your clients keep showing up just like they always did.

Price can define your difference

The business world is full of stories about products that sell because they're priced higher than others—they don't offer more, last longer, or work better; they're simply more expensive and so we *believe* they're somehow better.

You may not want to charge more for that reason alone, but remember that your price says something about you. Are you trying to be the cheapest, or are you offering a premium service? Regardless of your choice, you'll want to be sure that your rates consistently reflect your position.

What about lowering prices?

There's a tendency for CAM practices to operate as "boutique" businesses, providing a specialized service at a high price. This approach assumes that you offer something that people will pay extra for, that you have little competition, or that you can easily distinguish yourself from the competition.

There's nothing wrong, though, with considering the option of *lowering* your prices as a way to earn more. It may seem counter-intuitive, but lowering your prices can make your services more attractive to more people, resulting in more clients and more revenue.

In our clinic, patients initially started with a first visit lasting an hour, then came for a series of half-hour follow-up appointments. After some time, it became clear that half an hour wasn't always necessary—sometimes patients needed less time, and so we began to offer 15-minute visits that cost less than a half-hour did. The visits suited the clients, who were able to pay a little less (and perhaps come more often), but they also suited us. We could reach more people with the shorter visits, and because of the pricing, an hour of four short appointments created larger billings than an hour made up of two medium length ones.

There are other ways to lower your prices in order to grow your business, while still remaining profitable. We'll revisit this idea in the next chapter, but for now, hold on to the idea that the price of what you offer might be a lot more flexible than you think.

If you do change your prices, plan the transition in advance. While inflation never sleeps, you don't want to change your pricing too frequently. Once a year at the *most* is a good benchmark. Plan at least two rate hikes in advance—the current one and the next one. That strategy has helped us plan around office moves, sabbaticals and other significant events that we didn't necessarily want to associate with a fee hike.

Raising your prices is a good habit, but be sensible. Price hikes that don't reflect anything but your desire to charge more are eventually reflected in the desire your customers show for going elsewhere. Raising your fees every New Year's Day, for example, is predictable and unnecessary, and after a while your longstanding clients may come to see it as simply an annual cash grab.

Strategy #2. Add Products and services

While increasing your prices is an easy way to give yourself an instant pay raise, it's only going to take you so far. Plus, there's a lot to be said for not pricing yourself out of the market or out of the range of people who you might really wish to help. Raising your rates is simple, but it's not the only way to increase your revenue per visit.

Aranka Jones boosted her fledgling practice right from day one by adding other products and services to the mix.

"As a naturopath, building a steady income based on patient visits alone can take years—especially in a small town that is already home to four other NDs," she said. "By hiring an aesthetician, dedicating one of my treatment rooms to luxury eco-friendly spa treatments, and creating a retail space for high-end organic beauty products, I have created additional sources of income that generate revenue even while my patient load is light."

Aranka's goal to extend naturopathy into the beauty industry by detoxifying and "greening" the community, "one bathroom vanity at a time," did more than create a powerful crystal that defined her difference from other naturopaths. It allowed each of her clients to spend a little more in *her* practice, instead of elsewhere. Dollars that might have flowed to cosmetic aisles in pharmacies, for example, could now come to her practice instead.

Like Aranka, successful practitioners find ways to offer more to their customer base in order to get more revenue from the clients they have. And what's more, customers don't mind. If they've found a trusted source for the products and services they value, why *wouldn't* they want more?

How to choose a new offering

New services and products abound. It's easy to pick up a trade publication, visit a website, or go to a conference and find a new diagnostic tool, therapy, or supplement. Alternative health is big business.

Adding new offerings to your practice can help both you and your clients, but given the vast number of products and services out there, how do you choose? Here are four criteria you can use to evaluate new practice offerings:

Choose what's best for your clients

If you simply follow the rule of doing what's best for your clients, you'll rarely go wrong in selecting a new offering. Not only is it your obligation as a health care provider, but it really is the best way to create a healthy, lasting practice.

Choosing what's in the best interest of your client base requires that you ask yourself two questions. The first is, *Is there a conflict of interest?* For example, selling supplements might be considered a conflict—after all, the more you prescribe, the more you earn personally. That doesn't mean you can't do it, but an awareness of the issue will allow you to discuss it openly in your office and go a long way toward preventing its abuse—intentional or not. (In reality, just about everything in fee-for-service health care could be considered a conflict of interest. Your job is to be aware of it and draw your own lines.)

The second question you need to consider when choosing a new product or service is, *Does it work?* It's easy to jump on the bandwagon with the latest and greatest treatment tool or technique, but are you sure it really works? Is there evidence to support it? Have you tried it yourself? Have you tried it on a select group of trusted clients? Having to withdraw a new product or service after six months because it doesn't live up to its hype is both expensive and embarrassing.

Choose a fit

Closely related to choosing what's best for your clients is to choose something that *fits*. Does selling weight loss supplements *really* fit with your Asian medicine practice? Will that new health assessment test *really* appeal to your yoga clients? Only you can decide, but what's important is to ask the question.

Heather Furby offered one-on-one bodywork sessions to her workout groups and found that many took her up on the offer. "They already trust me in terms of their weightlifting workout, so now I can help them unwind the injuries that are obstacles to their workout goals. It also makes them feel special because I am only offering it to the exercise groups."

Choose something that attracts new clients

While the principle behind adding new products and services is to generate additional revenue from your current clients, it can have a profound effect in other ways. New products and services can also attract new clients and entice old ones to return.

Think outside of your modality when considering new products and services. If you're a massage therapist, can you add an infrared sauna? As a chiropractor, can you sell supplements? For your own modality, what about testing or diagnostics? Adding new treatments? Selling books and videos?

Not only do these give your existing clients more choice, but they also expand your possible market of new clients.

While a new product or service might provide a great opportunity to reach a whole new group that you haven't before, be sure that it doesn't interfere with your core clientele and the sparkling crystal that defines your difference.

Choose profitability

You need to make a profit on what you sell. Nothing will bring you to a standstill on the path to Success faster than losing money.

One offering can be more profitable than another based on its cost, what clients will pay, how long it takes, who administers it, and how often it can be repeated. All other things being equal, it makes sense to offer profitable products and services over unprofitable ones. The trick, of course, is to *know*.

Make sure you look at *all* the costs of your new offering. Will it take more time? Supplies you hadn't considered? Repairs? Does it require more insurance, maintenance or space?

Our experience is that things often have hidden costs, and the single best way to discover them in advance is to simply ask someone else who's already offering it.

Choose something that takes no time

The challenge in adding services in particular is that you might not have time to actually *do* them, or that they're not profitable enough to make it worth your time.

Before you give up on the idea, though, ask yourself whether there's something that clients can do themselves. Many treatments from saunas to colonics and inhalation therapies can be self-directed with minimal time on the part of the practitioner. (Of course, you can also choose something that *another* practitioner can do, but more on that later.)

Choose a different focus: Practitioner-driven vs. client-driven treatments

As we mentioned in the last chapter, practitioner-driven treatments are done almost entirely by the practitioner *for* the clients. Things like massage, chiropractic, and acupuncture are great examples. The client arrives, is treated, and leaves.

If you are heavily client-driven—that is, you use a lot of therapies that require your client to do the work—then you might consider adding something practitioner-driven to the mix. Just remember that our goal is to increase revenue per *visit*, not create more visits as we did with the first lever.

Strategy #3: Bundle

Once you've added more to your practice to increase your revenue per visit, it can be helpful to change the way you sell your products and services. "Bundling" is one strategy to help your clients use more of the products and services you offer than they might otherwise.

A bundle is a collection or grouping of products and services that targets a particular outcome, benefit, or condition. When your home phone company offers you internet access and cell phone service as well, it's bundling together several offerings to get more of your dollars. When a furniture store sells you a sofa, plus a special fabric treatment, delivery, and an extended warranty for one price, that's bundling. It's taking the $1,000 sofa you would have bought anyway and sticking it in a package with other things for a total of $1,200 so that you spend more.

But bundles don't have to be evil marketing tools. If your phone company can save you money by offering cell service, internet service, *and* home phone service for one price, then you can spend less, pay one easy bill, and have a single point of contact. The result is a bundle is great for everyone.

Bundles do one of two things: they either increase the amount a person spends on health care, or they shift some of the money a client is already spending somewhere else into your practice. They're attractive to clients because they offer a *solution to a problem*, and done correctly, can save clients money, too.

A massage therapist might sell a stress-reduction protocol, for example, that includes:

- A stress assessment test or questionnaire.
- A series of massage treatments using a mixture of techniques.
- A relaxation CD or mp3 soundtrack.
- A workshop on time management.

A massage isn't a solution. It's simply what you *do*. But a stress-reduction bundle? Now that's a solution to a problem, and clients love solutions to problems. At the same time, your client is spending more money with you. It's win-win.

Bundles are also a great opportunity to partner. You may have an idea for a bundle but you might lack some of the skills, facilities, resources, or interest for offering the whole thing. If that's the case, maybe someone *else* can offer part of it. You can work together to promote it, reaching more people and building a referral bridge while you're at it.

BEYOND THE SECOND LEVER

Getting people across the river is an investment. It takes time and energy to expand your market. Once you've got them across, though, offering them more doesn't take nearly as much effort. That's the power of the second lever: getting more from existing clients is far easier than finding new ones.

But it's not just about "getting more." If you've done your job right and chosen a new product or service that's a fit and is effective, then you're not just getting more, you're *giving* more, too—and that's where the great joy of Success lies: at the intersection of what's good for you the practitioner, what's good for your practice, and what's good for your patients.

It's not that difficult to have each of your clients help shift the figurative boulder by using the second lever. Each little push might not be much, but the cumulative total of all the incremental shifts in the boulder can really start to clear the path.

But what if it's not enough? Imagine that your practice *is* busy—you're seeing a steady stream of new and return clients. As you work with each client, you know that you're offering the best care you can, and they're happy to pay for it.

But there's just one catch: you're really busy. Really, *really* busy. And the phone just keeps ringing. What's next? How do you stay balanced and keep growing?

7. The Third Lever

If you want to empower people, put more clients than providers in the room.[3]

-Dr. Michael O. Smith, MD, DAc

*I*f you put the first two levers to work, the boulder that's been blocking the path to Success will shift dramatically. Getting your clients to come back and getting them to spend more will take you a long way. In fact, those first two forms of leverage might move the boulder just enough so that you can slip by and continue on the path.

There's still a bottleneck in the road, though. As we attract more clients, get them to come back more often, and offer them increased services, things also get busier. Remember Josh, the Asian medicine practitioner? He's fully booked. To do anything more than raise his prices and add a few products to his office requires that he work more, and he's not willing to make that sacrifice. He's busy enough. But saying "no" means confronting that nasty feeling of turning people away even though he *knows* he can help them. Josh, like many of us, became a practitioner to say "yes" to helping, not "no."

It also means that his income is essentially frozen in place for the rest of his career, which bothers him even though he loves what he's doing. Josh, like most of us, has a few dreams that involve some extra money—a retirement, some travel, giving more to charity, and sending his kids to college, to name a few.

If you asked Josh, he'd say he's got that funny "stuck" feeling, like he's running in place. He's working hard, he's good at what he does, and his practice is financially successful. But he's still not making the progress he'd like.

Josh needs to move the boulder a little more. He still can't quite squeeze past. He can see the path ahead as clear as day—it's almost as if he can reach out and touch it—but he can't *get* there.

It's a frustrating spot. When the day arrives for you, as it inevitably will, how do you continue to reach toward success while still helping the clients who are piling up behind you, and do it all without compromising your own balance? It's easy to say that you'll just close your practice to new clients, but that can be easier said than done for those of us who've chosen a career in healing. What's more likely to happen is that you'll add just one more client. Then another. Gradually your sense of balance will slip away and that vision of Success that seemed so close will begin to recede into the distance while Burnout draws ever nearer.

What to do? Fortunately our Greek friend Archimedes is still offering more options for our seesaw lever. There's a new leverage point that allows us to move the boulder even further without expanding beyond solo practice.

Let's recap the most recent legs of the journey. We've attracted new clients from across the river. They're helping push the boulder (returning more often), and they're pushing *harder* by spending a little more on other helpful, appropriate products and services.

But what if we had them push *together?*

Jordan Van Voast, a licensed acupuncturist in Seattle, was commuting 400 miles a week to practice in his boutique-style acupuncture clinic. Despite the long drive and occasionally harrowing winter moment, however, commuting wasn't the only problem on Jordan's mind. Lately, he'd been experiencing an ethical disconnect in the way he was practicing.

Jordan was discovering one of the uncomfortable truths of fee-for-service care: it excludes vast numbers of people who don't have pricey insurance plans or can't afford large out-of-pocket fees. "Boutique" is a term sometimes used for one-on-one practices that tend to be priced for people with incomes in the upper middle-class range or higher. Jordan's practice fit squarely into that category.

During a visit to New Orleans, however, he encountered something very different: acupuncture being delivered to groups of multiple people at the same time. "New Orleans was post-disaster," said Jordan, "And the acupuncture was more akin to a government-sponsored free clinic. But the experience of seeing traumatized people heal in groups had a deep effect on me."

What Jordan was seeing was an entirely different model for delivering care called community acupuncture (CA). It wasn't long before he was enrolled in a community acupuncture work-shop offered by Working Class Acupuncture, the brainchild of CA founder Lisa Rohleder, LAc.

Lisa started Working Class Acupuncture with the audacious idea that acupuncture really could be priced at a fraction of what typical boutique practices charged.[4] After watching her fellow practitioners go out of business in droves trying to service the small slice of the population that could afford expensive one-on-one visits, Lisa built a new business model for acupuncture from the ground up—one that allowed for more accessibility and more frequent visits.

In order to charge less, but still earn a living, Lisa's strategy was to treat multiple clients at the same time. Working Class Acupuncture practitioners see three to eight clients at once. The clients are treated simultaneously in recliners instead of one at a time on full treatment tables (although they do have tables available as needed). Clients not only pay an average of less than a third of what they would for a typical boutique acupuncture visit, but they also pay on a sliding scale, meaning they actually *choose* the amount they pay.

The end result is more accessible health care, practitioners who can earn a living, and a business that is decidedly different from those around it. As Lisa says, "People who like their acu-puncture to be upscale can easily differentiate themselves from those of us who choose to do simple treatments in community settings."[5] In fact, Working Class Acupuncture itself has other boutique acupuncturists practicing successfully in the same office. In essence, they're not even competitors.

There are now CA clinics around the world offering acupuncture at prices well below what boutique practices charge. They're people like Jordan, who have decided that there's another way to deliver care that serves the practitioner, the practice, *and* makes treatment available to people who would never have been able to afford it otherwise. As Jordan said, "We're only taught to treat the upper-middle class." Putting more clients than practitioners in the room changes all that.

Jordan's shift in practice has given him the leverage he needed to start shifting the boulder out of his way. It's our third lever, and one that's applicable not just to acupuncture, but to almost any practice.[6]

THE THIRD LEVER: MORE CLIENTS AT ONCE

One-on-one treatment is the universal starting point for a vast majority of CAM practitioners. It's how we learn, and for most of us, it's how we first develop our practices. After all, many of the alternative health philosophies are grounded in an intimate understanding of the client as a unique individual, so it's only natural that a practitioner would treat one client at a time. But group treatment has a long history in many healing professions from chiropractic to counseling—and for good reason.

Lisa Rohleder's motivation was *accessibility*—she wanted to open acupuncture to a wider range of people but still allow acupuncturists to earn a living. Her vision was the democratization of acupuncture. But you don't need to feel the fire of revolution to put the advantages of the third lever to work and shift the boulder that's blocking your path to Success.

Group treatment offers other enticing benefits beyond accessibility, such as:

Money

The most obvious benefit for most practitioners is that they can make more with every hour of their time. Instead of seeing one client over the course of an hour, you could treat a dozen or more. That's time well spent.

Enhanced client experience

In Jordan's clinic, family groups often come in together and find comfort sitting side by side. But even for strangers, there's a surprising value in being together. "We're so used to seeking solitude and isolation—it's a knee jerk response to stress," says Jordan. "But there's value in finding relaxation, peace, and serenity in groups."

We see the same value in our own clinic's intravenous therapy room, where groups of patients interact while receiving IV treatments lasting up to an hour or more. There's camaraderie in groups, as well as a real sense of reassurance for clients with similar challenges in knowing they're not alone. As Jordan said, "We are social animals. [Clients are] much more comfortable when the room is full."

There's also evidence to suggest that group work is not only enjoyable for the clients, but that it's more effective. A review of research on group versus individual treatments for obesity, for example, found significantly greater weight change for group-based versus individual treatments.[7]

If your assumption is that treating multiple clients at once won't work as well, or that people won't like it, think again. Most practitioners working in groups will tell you quite the opposite.

Pricing flexibility

Seeing more clients at one time gives you far more flexibility in your pricing. If you'd like to lower your prices to make your services more accessible, appeal to a different target group, or compete in a busy market, then group treatments may be exactly what you need. Group work allows you to lower your prices without devaluing your time. If your price goes down but the volume of people you see goes up, then your workday will deliver the same (or more) revenue in the same amount of time.

Balance

With that increased effectiveness in the use of your time comes another benefit: you can keep your life balanced. As Manon Bolliger, naturopath, Bowen therapist, and founder of Bowen College says of working with multiple clients, "Instead of working five days a week, you can work three."

That simple truth is no small thing. Working with multiple clients at once can leave you with more time for you, your family, your community, and your own health.

Options

Manon Bolliger didn't start off seeking balance, though. She found herself with no choice but to put the third lever to work. "When I started out, all I could afford was to rent one treatment room and a waiting room," she said. "I had no choice but to work with more than one person at a time."

Bowen therapy is one of several types of care that require short periods of "downtime" between practitioner actions. The one or two minutes between Bowen movements, for example, become difficult to use—they're too short to get into something else, and many practitioners find it difficult to stay focused while simply "waiting around" for the next step. Working with multiple clients eliminates the downtime, making their time more effective.

Working with multiple clients at once is "simply necessary in a lot of cases," says Amber Korobkina, Bowen therapist and founder of Let it Heal Clinics. "You don't know how long a session will last. Some clients will be there for three hours, especially when we get into the mind-body stuff. They fall asleep. We make sure that we can make that happen when they need it."

Group work can also be done online or by phone. It's the model that many practitioners—particularly those who deal in nutrition, lifestyle coaching, and counseling—are switching to. With little overhead, some help from technology, and a good contact list, practitioners are taking their skills and experience online into group classes that aren't restricted by the costs and limitations of physical space.

Group treatment online (just like in the real world) is highly scalable. It often costs little or nothing to add another client to a group treatment model. This means that each additional client is highly profitable, which in turn gives you even *more* options.

The third lever, in other words, does more than just move the boulder. It builds flexibility in how and where you practice, how much you work, and what you need to charge to make a living.

MAKING GROUP TREATMENT WORK

While group treatment carries huge advantages for your practice (and your life), it's a different creature from working one-on-one.

Your immediate reaction to the idea may be to dismiss it. Depending on your philosophy and your profession, you may consider the idea of treating more than one client at a time to be impossible or, at best, impractical. That's fine—there's no need to use this lever. You don't *have* to treat multiple clients at once, but it's a powerful way to earn more, help more, and be more accessible at the same time.

Remember, you can still work with clients individually. You don't have to change your entire practice to group treatment, and you don't need a full practice to start doing it. If you do decide to put the third lever to work in your practice, here are a few tips:

Finding your group treatment

Treating more than one client at a time can be done in one of two ways.

Shared care provides one-on-one treatment similar to how it would be done in a single-client setting, but multiple clients share the practitioner's personal attention. Examples of this are multiple clients receiving acupuncture, chiropractic, IV therapy, or energy-related touch treatments. The practitioner divides her time between clients and monitors, treats, and modifies as needed. The treatment is essentially one-on-one, but all clients are in a shared space (or, alternatively, in semi-separate rooms or treatment areas) and undergoing care more or less simultaneously.

Group care is a one-to-many approach where all participants receive the same treatment at the same time. This is the model used in group therapy, and it can also be applied in the form of educational talks, health workshops, activity- and fitness-based classes, guided meditation, and imagery sessions. It's why that yoga class you attend might only cost a few dollars a session, but the instructor or studio owner can still make a living by putting ten, twenty, or more clients in the room at the same time.

Both types of treatments do essentially the same thing: they bring clients together to push in unison on the boulder in a win-win scenario for the clients and the practitioner.

There are two distinct questions you need to ask in order to find your first (or next) group treatment. The first is aimed inward, and it forms the basis of this chapter: *How can I do what I do now, but with more people at once?*

In other words, how can you take your current form of interacting with clients and do it with a roomful of clients at the same time?

To get the most from this first question, you really need to challenge your thinking. Your knee-jerk reaction may well be, "I can't," and you might just be right. But push it a little bit further. Are you *sure* about that?

Any type of counseling treatment, from psychotherapy to nutrition, can be done in a group setting. Chiropractors can work in rooms full of tables, moving from client to client, or (as many already do) moving from room to room. Acupuncture, as we've seen, can be done in communal rooms. Bowen therapy and spa treatments, IV treatments, weight loss and lifestyle counseling—they can all be done in settings that involve more clients than practitioners.

Remember that your group treatment offering doesn't have to be *identical* to the one-on-one version. Don't get too caught up in the way you currently do things. Community acupuncture isn't the same as boutique, but it works. What's more, it can be profitable, carve out a great niche, and give access to people who might not normally be able to afford acupuncture at all.

Of course, sometimes treating multiple people at once just doesn't work. We have a colon hydrotherapy suite in our clinic, and as you can imagine, colon cleansing in a group setting is a tough sell. We can still educate clients in groups on the value of digestive health and detoxification, but the actual colonic treatment will likely always be a one-on-one experience.

What do you do if you just can't see how your treatment could become a group treatment? If that's the case, then move on to the second question: *What group treatment can I <u>add</u> to my current offering?*

Just because your current practice doesn't lend itself to group treatment doesn't mean that you can't add something that does. Go back to the second lever for some ideas on adding new services. Start asking practitioners in other professions about what they do, or talk to clients who may have experienced care in other ways. As a massage therapist, for example, can you add group stress reduction, or multi-client energy treatments to your practice? If what you do simply doesn't fit the group model, there's always something similar that will.

Finding space

Because so many practitioners operate in small solo offices, the first hurdle of group treatment is often simply finding the space to do it. It's easy to think, "I don't have the space, so I can't do it unless I move. And I'm not ready to move, so that's that."

Consider starting small. You might find it easiest to try a tiny test group that you can work with in your current space. We started our group IV suite in a relatively small room, and once we realized how great the experience was, we expanded into a larger space. Don't be afraid to just *try*. Move the furniture. Get creative. Experiment a bit before you dismiss the idea altogether.

Just like clients crossing the river, you may need a stepping stone that lets you experience group treatment with as little risk as possible.

Convincing your clients

Even if they have the space, many practitioners are concerned about how their clients will respond to group treatment. In our culture, health care is predominantly a solo mission on the part of the client. When clients do encounter each other, it's often because they're forced to do it in waiting rooms or other uncomfortable surroundings. Because so much of CAM is focused on boutique practices, many practitioners worry that people will be turned off by sharing time, space, and attention with others.

But in reality, clients come to love the camaraderie offered by group treatments. If you do need to convince your clients, here are a few talking points:

- *It's effective.* As mentioned, group work is good stuff. It really works.
- *It's cheaper.* Group work lets you keep your prices lower. Most clients appreciate that.
- *It builds a community.* Discovering other people who may be on similar healing journeys can be a powerful and highly beneficial experience.
- *It's available.* Group treatment allows you see many more people in one appointment slot, creating more convenience for clients in choosing treatment times.

Some clinics offer both group and private treatments. The combination is a way of making sure that those people who want the personalized attention don't fall through the cracks. Whether or not you choose to do both is up to you.

For us, group treatments are more than just an efficient way to deliver care—they're a philosophy of care that goes beyond simple economics. Clients in our clinic get plenty of one-on-one time with practitioners, but there are certain treatments that are just done in groups, period. We could charge more and offer private sessions, but we'd lose something along the way, too.

Easing in

Nearly every practitioner we spoke to about working with multiple clients at once had the same advice for newcomers: *start slowly.*

"The most important thing when working with multiple clients is to ease into it," said Amber Korobkina. "Start with one, and gradually add another person here and there. Never jump in with both feet. Ease in. You have to know what your limits are. There are times when you have to say 'no.'"

Likewise, remember that even in groups, people are still people. To treat them like a herd doesn't make for a sustainable practice. "It's not drive-through Bowen," says Amber. "You don't want to rush. It's still an experience for the client. Even if that person only sees you for two minutes at a time, you need to be fully present."

The third lever offers great advantages. Just be sure to use them wisely.

THE POWER OF THE THREE LEVERS

Even with our three levers, it can take a lot of effort to move the boulder. In fact, it can at times feel as if you're pushing the boulder *uphill.* The good news, though, is that once you reach the top of the hill, the boulder begins to gain its own momentum. You'll find that it gets increasingly easier to get past future barriers on the path.

If we look back on the last few chapters, we can see that they aren't just random thoughts on growing your practice. They're presented in a very specific sequence:

- Stepping stones and bridges deliver prospects and clients.
- The first lever gets them to keep coming back.
- The second lever gets them to spend more each visit.

- The third lever allows us to see more of them at once.

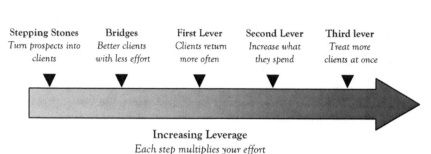

Increasing Leverage
Each step multiplies your effort

Most practice growth and marketing efforts are directed exclusively at the first two levels (stepping stones and bridges). You'd be surprised at how many practices spend enormous amounts of time and energy attracting new clients, while ignoring the ones they already have. They spend and spend and struggle and struggle, and clients continue to flow through their practices, never to return. It's draining and will eventually burn out a practitioner physically, emotionally, and financially.

You can pick and choose what levers you use in your practice, but to get the most from your practice, growth should be about leveraging *all* of these steps—about getting way out on that long seesaw lever where you can do more with less. Each step *multiplies* your efforts, building on the previous so you can get more from your practice without waking up one day to discover you've reached Burnout, not Success.

The levers are deceiving in their simplicity. Yes, they're easy concepts, but they can move mountains—or boulders, in our case. The simple process of getting clients, keeping them, delivering more to them, and then doing all of that for many of them at once is a powerful formula that will take your practice to new levels of success.

IDENTIFYING THE BOULDER

Being able to spot the boulder is critical to moving forward. Not only will it obstruct your ability to grow, but if you don't realize you're facing it, you'll find yourself spending increasing amounts of time and energy on bridges and stepping stones in an effort to find new clients—a process that will guide you slowly but surely toward No Longer Practicing. Remember Karen from the beginning of this section? She was slowly burning out trying to keep up the flow of new patients into her practice.

The boulder in our story is pretty easy to spot: it's a huge rock. Realizing that you're facing the boulder in practice, though, can be a little trickier. Like Karen, you'll know you're facing the boulder if any of the following are true:

- You see new clients once or twice, but rarely more.
- Once you help resolve a client's initial concern, you're unlikely to see him again.
- You don't communicate with your clients about things other than their current treatment details like appointment reminders and billing issues.
- You're still charging the same rates you were three or more years ago.
- You only sell one basic service and its price is based on your time.
- You rarely, if ever, add more products or services to what you offer.
- Your average revenue per visit is well under that of your colleagues in similar practices.
- Your average annual revenue per *patient* is lower than colleagues in similar practice
- You feel as though you'd like to earn more but think the only way to do it is to work more hours.

Any of these is an indicator that, at least to some extent, your path to Success is being blocked by a boulder that you can't move without one of the levers.

Put the three levers to work and the boulders that crop up on the path will be easy to deal with. But is that it? If the path is well marked and the way is clear, do we just push on ahead to Success?

Let's head back to the path to find out.

INSIGHTS FROM THE BOULDER

The boulder is what keeps your practice from growing even when you have a steady supply of new clients.

To shift the boulder, you have three levers at your disposal:

THE FIRST LEVER

More return visits to your practice mean you can spend less time and money seeking new clients.

THE SECOND LEVER

When your clients spend more each time they return to your practice, you earn more without working more.

THE THIRD LEVER

Treating multiple clients at once lets you to help more and earn more without burning out.

PART IV: THE VALLEY
Finding Balance and Building a Sustainable Career

Over every mountain there is a path, although it may not be seen from the valley.

-Theodore Roethke

hen the realization dawns on you, it arrives as a bit of a shock: the path is getting easier. Or you're getting better at walking it. Which one is true you're not sure, but the fact remains that you're making good progress.

People are crossing the river daily, now. Some cross on stepping stones, but even more are crossing on bridges. It has become rare that you're alone.

The boulder lies far behind you, and as people return more often to visit you on the path, you find your spirits soaring. You're now able to help more people in a day than you might have in a month back when you started your journey.

The path is clear, for the most part—even the occasional rocks you find blocking the way are easily cleared by the sheer volume and commitment of your companions. Your days are beginning to look a lot like what you imagined they might when you first began this journey.

One day, you and your companions reach the top of a ridge. Looking back, you can see the trail of people following behind, crossing back and forth across the many bridges you've created along the way. It's an inspiring sight, and you take a few moments to enjoy the view before following the path back into the forest.

Just a short while later, though, the trees part and you find yourself staring in wonder at a new vista before you.

The forest has given way to the high rock walls of a majestic valley. The sand beneath your feet, you realize, was once part of an ancient riverbed. You stand in awe of the valley, gazing up at its towering walls. Beautiful waterfalls tumble thousands of feet down to the valley floor where their mist has created a fertile valley filled with remarkable flowers and fruit trees. It's truly a paradise—a hidden garden virtually untouched by human passage. In fact, the only sign you can see that anyone has been here before you is a very faint trail leading off toward the end of the valley.

This place is more beautiful than any you've ever seen. It's the perfect place to finally end your journey. The perfect place to live, to help others, and to enjoy what you've traveled so far to do. The bridges are built, the path has been cleared of boulders, and the people are finding their way to you.

This, you realize, is *it*. You've arrived at Success.

As your gaze drifts toward the end of the valley, you see that the faint footpath ends up ahead. After following it a short way, you discover that a section of the high cliff wall has collapsed and an massive rockslide has blocked off the entire end of the valley.

As you draw closer to the rockslide, you grasp just how enormous it is. It's as if someone has taken thousands of the huge boulders you worked so hard to move from the trail and dumped them all in one spot.

As you take in the scale of the landslide, the sun begins to sink behind the rock walls and a beautiful sunset spreads through the valley.

What luck, you think. *That landslide could have destroyed Success.*

You sigh in relief, take a breath of crisp, fresh air, and gaze at the incredible beauty around you.

You've finally arrived.

Once you're settled, the days pass quickly. As people enter the valley, you fall into an easy rhythm of helping and healing. One day you realize that *you're really good at this.* The sense of uncertainty from earlier in the journey has vanished, and you begin to work with increased confidence, secure in your knowledge and your skills. Each day, you wake up inspired by the beauty around you and the joy of being able to help others.

As you work, word spreads of a magnificent place where a powerful healer helps people by the thousands. More people begin to arrive in the valley. *I'm successful,* you think. *I've made it!*

One morning you wake at dawn and walk toward the base of the falls to have a cool drink and a swim before your work begins. It's become your favorite way to start the day.

You've only taken a few steps in the half-light of morning, however, when someone approaches. "Could you help me?" she asks. You glance at the waterfall in the distance for a moment, but then decide that it can wait. You smile warmly and invite the stranger to sit.

Later, after you've been able to help the grateful stranger, you head off toward the falls again. You've only gone a few paces, though, when you're stopped once more by another new face.

As you speak with the new stranger, another person arrives in the valley. Then another. *I'll get to the falls at the end of the day,* you think. *It's going to be a busy one.*

It's near sunset when you finish up. You're exhausted, and you skip your trip to the falls, promising yourself that you'll go tomorrow. But by sunrise the next morning, there are even *more* people waiting for you. It's another busy day.

And then another.

And another.

A few weeks pass and you realize that this isn't temporary—there are more and more people arriving every day. You resolve to get up an hour earlier in the morning to ensure you have time to visit the falls for your meditative swim.

In the pre-dawn darkness, you shuffle wearily down the path, tired but looking forward to a return to your morning routine.

When you reach the falls, though, you can't believe your eyes: even in the faint light of morning you can see the water is filthy.

In fact, the whole place has changed. The grass and flowers have been trampled by crowds of people. The water is cloudy and littered with garbage. The animals that used to share the water with you have vanished. The birds, too, have gone silent.

What was once a paradise is quickly becoming a wasteland.

As you look around in shock, you hear the commotion of yet another group of people pouring into the valley. You feel the urge to clean up. To slow the tide of new faces. To do *something*.

But you can't. There are people who need your help.

With a sigh you turn your back on the falls and walk slowly toward the voices in the distance.

❋

A decade after opening his doors, Gabe had created a multi-million-dollar practice. His clinic had more than a dozen practitioners, and clients traveled from distant points for his care. His efforts had rewarded him well. His generous income funded his beachfront home, boat, cars, vacations, and a solid financial future for his children.

It had also made him prematurely gray, chronically ill, and now, after having come so far, he was on the edge of a nervous breakdown. The debt he'd acquired to grow his business so quickly had to be serviced. Clients needed to be treated. Staff needed to be managed.

Under pressure to keep cash flow pouring into his practice, he worked more. His health deteriorated further and his family relationships began to decay.

As Gabe described it:

"You've invested in your future, but you have to pay for that investment. The more you have to work to pay for that investment, the less time you have to spend with your family. Then when you do spend time with them, you feel guilty for not spending more, or for not being at work trying to catch up.

"What little time you are home you spend fighting with them because you haven't been home. You find yourself just wishing you were back at the office, working."

On the path to Success, Gabe had found himself mired in something that just *looked* like it. Gabe was deep in the valley and he had no idea how to cope. But things would get worse for him before they got better. In the end, the valley would almost cost Gabe his life.

"Eventually, I started to wonder: would this be easier for them if I wasn't here? You find yourself looking at your life insurance, wondering if it might be better if you weren't around. That's when you realize you've become a patient. You've crossed the line from helping to needing help."

That's when you realize you've become a patient. Powerful words, and the best possible description of what happens to practitioners who can't manage life in the valley. Many may not reach the depth of Gabe's despair, but everyone who fails to deal with the challenge of the valley suffers in some way.

What's most poignant about Gabe's situation, though, is that *it's what so many practitioners think they want.* They dream of a day when they have all the clients they need and can simply do the work of providing care without worrying about how to pay the bills or find new clients. It's a dream of days free of risk, struggle, and worry.

The valley in our story is that dream—a place of security and consistency where everything is predictable. It's the point in a practice where clients arrive steadily and your services are in high demand. Perhaps you're booked weeks or even months in advance. You don't worry much about paying the bills because there's a never-ending line of people waiting to give you more to do. For many practitioners, the valley is the goal: a steady supply of clients, beautiful surroundings, and a predictable routine each day. It's what most so many of us wish for.

But for all its beauty, the valley can be a tough spot to stay. You can see where the story is taking us. Soon enough, the valley will be filled with thousands of people. The water will be sullied, the flowers trampled, and you'll be under enormous pressure to deal with each and every one of those people on a personal basis.

As your practice grows—which it will—there will come a point when you reach the valley. You may not recognize it when it happens, but one day you'll notice that you've stopped worrying about where to find more clients and started worrying about where to find the time to *treat* them. You'll begin to wonder if you've reached Success, or if you've simply arrived at Burnout.

The valley is a paradox in the growth of your practice. It's having enough clients to finally pay the bills, but suddenly having no time to enjoy the fruits of your labors. It's the joy of helping others with their health, coupled with the pain of losing yours. It's the comfort of a steady schedule, offset by the dead end feeling that you can't take time off when you need it.

The high walls of the valley can provide safety and security, but they can also be a prison keeping you from growing and moving forward. In other words, the valley can look a lot like Success, but it can turn into Burnout without you realizing it.

The challenge presented by the valley is twofold. The first challenge is **how do you protect your own balance, health, and sanity while facing the increasing pressures of a busy practice?**

The second challenge is something different. Just about everything in *The Practitioner's Journey* so far is designed to get the solo practitioner closer to Success. But the valley is something new altogether. It's about making a *choice*. It's about deciding whether to remain a solo practitioner or to transform into something different.

The question of whether or not leave the valley is the kind of question we all tend to dislike: the kind with no right answer. At least, not one right answer for everyone. Just a right answer for *you*.

The next two chapters are about the two challenges faced by practitioners in the valley. The first is about how to stay sane, healthy, and balanced in the valley of solo practice—that is, how to transform the valley *into* Success. After all, it really can be a beautiful place. The second is about leaving the valley to find Success by transforming your solo practice into a health care *business*.

8. Lines in the Sand

"Moderate effort over a long time is important, no matter what you are trying to do. One brings failure on oneself by working extremely hard at the beginning, attempting to do too much, and then giving it all up after a short time."

-The Dalai Lama

*I*n Greek mythology (yes, more Greek), Procrustes was the son of the god Poseidon. He kept a home in the hills near Eleusis and would offer road-weary travelers an opportunity to kick back and recharge their batteries.

Procrustes was particularly proud of one thing in his home: a remarkable bed, which exactly matched the person who lay on it. For those on the road in ancient times, you can imagine that a good meal and a perfect-sized bed was a pretty appealing offer.

But Procrustes' hospitality was considerably less appealing than it sounds, and his bed was most decidedly *unremarkable*. It did indeed fit every person who lay on it, but only because Procrustes would either stretch him or cut his legs to length. Procrustes, it seems, was nothing more than a bandit, and Theseus, the famed Greek hero, would eventually "fit" Procrustes to his own bed by cutting off the tyrant's head and feet.

That was the end of the bandit, but not the end of his approach. One of the pitfalls of building a great practice and helping innumerable clients find their way to health is that your practice can become a Procrustean bed. The demands of a busy client base can painfully contort us, stretching our abilities, chopping off our personal time, and straining our commitments.

When you're not as busy as you'd like to be, it may seem that a demanding practice would be a great problem to have—being stretched to fit your practice bed seems like a great idea. But when you're overwhelmed and your health or personal life begins to suffer, that bigger bed starts to become a painful stretching rack. Before long, you're wishing desperately to return to a time when things were smaller and less complicated.

You can't find your way to sustainable Success without balance, and a practice that has become a Procrustean bed that tortures its practitioner to meet its changing size is anything but balanced. What follows is about ensuring that your practice is a comfortable bed that fits *you*, not the other way around. It's about becoming the Theseus in the legend, not the road-weary traveler who's been cut down to size or stretched beyond her breaking point.

THE SAND LINES: FINDING BALANCE

If you're struggling to find enough clients to pay the bills, it can be difficult to imagine a day when there might be *too many* clients or when your practice could negatively impact your own health. Likewise, it can be difficult to comprehend that you won't always be able to offer help to everyone who asks.

But practices *do* grow. Client success breeds practice success, which in turn breeds more client success. The phone begins to ring more and more, and then suddenly it's ringing almost constantly. Clients beg and plead, and turning off the phone or flipping the sign in the window to "Closed" begins to feel like an indictable offense. And vacations? They become full-blown acts of treason.

As your practice grows, you'll find yourself increasingly pressed, pressured, pushed, and prodded to do one thing more than anything else: *work*. The pressure will come from clients, from bills to pay, from colleagues, and (in no small part) from a culture that accepts that 50-hour workweeks are normal.

But in the end, most of the pressure will come from *you*. As Carl Honoré writes in his book *In Praise of Slow*, "Often the barrier to work-life balance is self-inflicted," and nowhere is this truer than in health care. The drive to heal, to help, and to *give* is strong in practitioners. And although that drive is part of what makes you exceptional at what you do, you need to make sure that the same drive doesn't drive you into the ground.

As a CAM practitioner, you're facing a *double* challenge. If anyone has a harder time finding balance and saying "no" than a health professional, it's a small business owner. The fact that you wear both of these hats puts you in the high-risk group for a one-way ticket to Burnout. If your empathy doesn't get you, then your business efforts will.

So how do you stay balanced? Let's start with three things we know for sure:

Balance is critical for you and your clients

If you suffer, so will the quality of care that your clients receive. As Gabe learned, you can't expect to lose balance and still keep your health, relationships, and practice intact.

Balance requires a conscious effort

Balance doesn't come built-in or pre-wrapped. It's a skill and it requires time and energy to find and maintain it.

It starts now

If you can't balance your life in a moderately busy practice, then a really busy one can chew you up. Finding balance is a skill best learned *before* we need it.

The good news is that you really can learn all the skills you need to stay balanced in a busy practice. Our tool for finding balance is as simple as it is ancient: a line in the sand.

In the time of the Roman Empire (it's about time we left Greece, really), a Macedonian king with a cash flow problem decided to invade Egypt. At the time, Egypt was under the protection of the mighty Roman army, so the Macedonians expected resistance and came prepared.

When the Macedonian army arrived at the border, however, they were met not by legions of Roman troops, but by a lone Roman senator named Laenus.

Legend has it that Laenus did something most unusual. He drew a circle in the sand around the Macedonian king and demanded that before the king stepped from the circle, he must agree to withdraw his army. The Macedonian king, awed by the bravery and confidence of Laenus and the Roman Empire, agreed.[8]

The story has survived to modern day in the expression "to draw a line in the sand," meaning to create a boundary that must not be crossed without careful consideration or dire consequence. It's a metaphor for an ultimatum, and it's the very tool we need to ensure that you and your practice stay in balance. We'll use it to draw three clear lines in the sand around your practice to protect your balance—and to preserve the beauty of the valley of private practice.

At the core of these lines in the sand is a clear message: *these are the things that are the most important to me, and they come first.* The sand lines are about clarifying your values and ensuring that your practice meets *your* needs first and foremost.

The three lines in the sand you'll need to draw are:

- *Time.* Effectively manage the time it takes to run a practice, see clients, *grow* a practice, and still have a life.
- *Money.* Take control of your finances in order to keep your time balance intact.
- *Healing.* Ensure that you can continue to treat clients with passion and joy—without sacrificing your own health and energy.

We'll look at specific strategies for creating and maintaining each boundary, and then examine what it means when we cross them.

THE FIRST LINE IN THE SAND: TIME

There is no commodity more precious in your life than time. Just about everything else in life can be bought, built, achieved, reclaimed, or recovered in some way, but time just keeps disappearing from our lives in an endless ribbon. Every minute that slips by is gone and there's no getting it back.

If that seems grim, don't be disheartened. That same passage of time is what gives us wisdom, deep relationships, financial abundance, and a thriving practice. But once it's gone, you don't get it back, and when it comes to our three areas of balance, time is the one that you need to dedicate yourself to with the most passion.

What follows are three practitioner-specific strategies for drawing and maintaining your line in the sand with respect to time.

Strategy #1: Make personal time a priority. For real.

Practices have a way of sneaking up on you. As you strive to move forward on the path, you can sacrifice a lot to the journey and not realize it. It's not uncommon to wake up one morning and realize that you're way out of balance. Or, ironically, to have your body shut down because your profession as a healer has compromised your life as a person.

For that reason, the first line we'll draw in the sand will be around your personal time. Your own life and health and happiness need to take precedence over the needs of your practice.

This isn't about prioritizing your to-do list. There is an endless supply of time management advice out there, in every format: books, videos, blogs, and workshops. And much of it is excellent. None, however, will work unless you decide that your time is more important than anything else.

It's easy to pay lip service to the value of your time. To make it *really* work you must consciously decide that your time is worth more than anything else by taking action.

Here are some specific actions you can take to draw your line in the sand to protect your time:

- Design your schedule not by deciding what hours you will work, but what hours you *won't*, and then protect that time carefully.
- Take time annually to schedule your holidays for the next year (or more). If you don't carve the time out, then your practice will eventually take it from you.
- Be careful when choosing hours. If you don't want to work weekends forever, don't start now. It's harder to take hours away than it is to add them.
- Take long breaks. A three-day weekend is not the same as two weeks. You're a health care practitioner, and you need to walk the talk. You have to take the time you need (and it's different for everyone) so that you can play the most important role in care: setting a great example.

In short, you need to draw a line around your personal time, and cross it at your peril.

And what if you feel that you already have too much to do and couldn't possibly carve out more time for yourself? The answer is easy: practitioners who are "too busy" simply need to carve out more time anyway. So book your holidays. Cut back your hours. Just do it, and discover how effective you can become. Our experience has been that most practitioners don't use their time effectively. And the best way to become more effective with your time is to have less of it.

Does this mean that you can never go the extra mile? Never work late to help a client in need, or never make an exception in your hours? No. It just means that in the big picture, *you* are more important than your practice. So yes, you can walk the path at night, figuratively speaking, but remember that doing it regularly increases your risk of becoming lost and walking in circles instead of getting closer to Success.

Strategy #2: Work less

In 1955, author Cyril Parkinson published a humorous essay in *The Economist* satirizing the inefficiency of government bureaucracy. Its main point—that work expands to fit the time available—became known as "Parkinson's Law." It basically states that the more time you have to do something, the longer it will take you to do that something.

In practice, that means that the longer you give yourself to do things like record keeping, paying bills, and other administrative tasks, the longer you'll take to actually *do* them.

To beat Parkinson's Law you need to restrict the time you spend in your office *not* seeing clients—the time you spend on non-billable tasks. It's common for practitioners to spend 40 to 60 hours a week (or more) in their clinics, yet only see clients for half of those hours. It's a recipe for imbalance. It means that even when your practice isn't earning much, you're still overworked.

Set your clinic hours and leave some time for business and administrative duties, but don't hang around the office if you don't have clients to see. Schedule your clients close together, and if you're not busy, *leave*. Your workload will expand to fit the time you have available, so *don't make it available*. You can do all your non-client work in five hours, ten hours, or 25 hours a week—it's your choice. Just remember, if you hang around the office all the time, it'll take... well, all of your time.

If you have trouble with this, make commitments at the end of your scheduled administrative time—make arrangements for social activities, family time or other obligations that will get you out of the office, and compartmentalize your administrative time.

Working less means restricting your client hours, too. Why offer 35 hours of client time a week if you're only 40 percent booked? You end up hanging around the office waiting for your next client and spending too much time on your admin work. If you're not heavily booked, restrict your client hours until you're closer to 70 percent full or more. Set a reasonable minimum number of office hours, and don't expand them until you actually need to.

If working less seems overly simplistic, don't be fooled. Try it and you'll see just how efficient you become. **What most practitioners miss out on is that they can almost always spend less time at work and earn the same amount.**

Strategy #3: Manage your book

The previous two strategies have less to do with managing your time and more to do with simply being stringent in how much of it you allow your practice to *have*. Once you've decided how much time you're going to allocate, you'll need to manage those hours.

As a practitioner, you sell your time for money. What controls that time is your appointment book. You might use a paper calendar to manage appointments or you might use a full-blown practice management software solution. You might use a simple computer calendar or you might use sheets of paper and a ruler. It's up to you. But every practitioner's professional life is controlled by the calendar.

At least, that's the common belief.

The truth is that you need to tame your appointment book with the same diligence you use to stop your professional life from running roughshod over your personal one.

During our interviews for *The Practitioner's Journey*, we stumbled across the most unusual scheduling process we've ever encountered. It's as inspiring as it is effective.

Sue Painter is a massage therapist and business coach in Tennessee. Her practice is not simply booked solid—it's booked solid *a year in advance*. That's right: with the exception of a three-day scheduling blitz in December, Sue spends no time on scheduling during the year. Her appointment book is rarely used other than to see who's next.

How does she do it? Early on, Sue realized that her clients frequently wanted the same time slots over and over. So every December, as soon as she starts to accept bookings for the upcoming year, she emails all her clients to let them know that the book is open. Then, "The emails pour in. I go through three days of agony fitting everyone in for the year, but then it's done. It saves me so much time. It's so much faster for them and me."

Sue's system cuts an enormous amount of schedule management time out of her year. That leaves more time for *her*, an ingredient that she recognized as being essential early on in practice. And not only does her system cut down on the time she spends booking, but the scarcity of her appointments means she also has virtually no cancellations. "I have almost no no-shows. Clients will give their appointments away to a friend. They're filling my book for me."

Sue, like many successful practitioners, treats her time as a limited resource. She recognizes the limits of her workweek and so she sets limits on her bookings, creates scheduling boundaries that support those limits, and reaps the benefits. But don't miss the hidden bonus here: the benefits aren't just hers. Her clients are also happier. "They love it," Sue told us. "Clients say it helps them make massage a priority in their lives." By carefully managing her time and her book, Sue, in essence, is helping her clients do the same.

Sue's system is astoundingly effective. It may not work for you, but remember that booking clients ineffectively is a dangerous game in terms of balance. An ineffectively booked schedule generates a fraction of the revenue that a properly booked one does. That means your appointment book is not only critical to you income, but it's the single biggest factor in keeping your time balanced. Ineffective booking policies will keep you working longer hours for the same (or less) money and lead you on yet another shortcut to Burnout.

The good news is that managing your appointment book isn't difficult. It just requires that same line-in-the-sand commitment that we've applied to other areas of life. Even if your practice doesn't lend itself to booking a year's business at one time, here are a few effective strategies for managing your appointment book.

Eliminate islands

Islands are created by gaps between clients. They result from not scheduling appointments effectively. Book your clients back to back. You'll stay in the flow of providing care, you'll have more free time, and you'll earn the same income with far fewer office hours.

Use a waiting list

One of the drawbacks of a tight schedule is that clients may not get their ideal appointment times. The most coveted time slots disappear quickly, but if you use a waiting list, the inevitable cancellations and reschedules that occur in practice can be filled with people from the list. It's easy and works amazingly well.

Make reminder calls

When a client doesn't show up, that appointment slot is gone. Even a waiting list isn't much help for a last-minute no-show. Call, text, or email your clients to remind them. The time it takes to remind them is far less than the time you'll lose when they don't show up.

But what if you feel like you *can't* implement some of these strategies? What if you feel like you can't afford a vacation or less than a five- or six-day workweek? Then you need to examine the role that time's dark twin—money—plays in your life.

THE SECOND LINE IN THE SAND: MONEY

You've got your holidays booked. Your hours are sustainable. You've created boundaries around your time. Voila! Balance, right? Not *quite*. There's a flipside to the balance coin: money.

Nothing is more certain to throw your time balance out of whack than a *cash* imbalance—particularly when you don't have enough of it. Feeling cash-strapped is stressful, draining, and, even worse, it's self-perpetuating. Failing to achieve financial balance in your professional and personal life creates a slippery slope to future money issues.

A money imbalance does two specific things to your practice, both of which serve to make your balance *worse*. First, a shortage of cash forces you to work more. Because you're trading time for money, you'll have to learn to manage money or you'll find yourself under constant pressure to earn (and therefore work) more.

Second, your resulting increased workload reduces the time you spend working *on* your practice instead of *in* it and it makes you less likely to invest in the proper growth that this book is all about. That means you need to work harder to find new clients, they come back less often, and you're less efficient dealing with them. The result? You need to work even *more*.

What this all adds up to is one critical insight that forms the basis for thinking about money in terms of work-life balance: **Any decision you make about money in your practice or personal life is also a decision about time.**

A decision to buy a new car, for example, is also a decision about the additional time investment required to work to pay for that car. A decision to have a larger or more expensive office space is also a decision about time. This doesn't mean you shouldn't have a new car or a larger space; it simply means that money decisions in solo practice are also time decisions, plain and simple.

That means that spending money equals spending time. So how do we add this second ball into our juggling act? How do we find and maintain financial balance?

Again, the answer is *boundaries*. As with balancing time, we need to draw clear lines in the sand to define the role money plays in our lives. Here are the critical ones for you and your practice:

Strategy #1: Understand the money and happiness link

More specifically, understand that there *isn't* one—beyond a certain point, at least.

Study after study has shown that once you get beyond the poverty line, money doesn't buy happiness. The upper class is, for the most part, no happier than the middle class.

How is this relevant to balance in your practice? If you're striving to earn more and more money by selling off more and more of your time, and you're doing it because you think it'll make you happy, then you're headed nowhere you want to be. Welcome to the toll highway to Burnout. Welcome to Gabe's life of big homes, fancy cars, and constant thoughts of suicide.

This strategy is about *intent*. When faced with balance-challenging opportunities like expanding your hours, seeing more clients, working harder, or working longer, it's in your best interests to ask yourself, *why?* And if the answer is to make more money, then you need to keep prodding yourself until you reach the truth of the matter.

Most people always feel like they don't have enough money—yes, even wealthy people. It's up to you to decide what enough means to you.

Strategy#2: Spend less than you make

One of the dangerous side effects of running a successful practice is that you make more money. If that sounds like a problem you'd like to have, you might be right. Just make sure you think it over first. More cash flowing through your practice and into your life leads to spending more. Spending more leads to working harder to earn more. Earning more leads to spending more. And the cycle continues.

Nothing will bring more balance to your life than simply spending less than you earn, and this applies to both your personal life and your practice. For most practitioners, home and business finances are closely linked. Overspend at home and you'll overdraw on your practice. Overspend on your practice and you'll leave nothing to bring home. **Every financial decision that you make in your personal life will create a ripple through your professional life.** Good financial balance starts first at home, then at work.

If this means downsizing your life, trust us—it's worth the effort. Drive an older car. Live in a smaller home. Make your own lunch. The point is not that you shouldn't drive a nice car, but that you shouldn't drive a nice car that *you can't afford*. Want a big home? Grow your practice to the point that you can *really* afford it.

But here's a reality check. Most of us are already in over our heads, and there isn't much precedence out there for downsizing. We all know that it's just not that likely to happen. And if it is likely for you, it probably won't be this book that convinces you.

What you *can* do that's within the scope of what we're talking about, however, is to put your lifestyle creep on hold.

"Lifestyle creep" is the tendency for your life to gradually become more expensive to maintain over time. It's perfectly normal—after all, most of us don't really want to live like students our whole lives. Plus, when you start adding a family to the picture, life can become more costly.

The danger of lifestyle creep is that upward trend in our consumption often outstrips the upward trend in our *income*. Ever wonder how people making millions of dollars per year can spend all their money? It's not as hard as you think, and that slow upward creep is partly responsible. It may seem inconceivable to you now that you could earn ten times your current income and *still* be short of cash or in debt, but you'd better believe that it's more than possible; it's happening right now to your neighbours, your colleagues and your friends.

Just because it's normal, though, doesn't mean you need to give in to it. If you can't spend less than you make right now, then at least commit to putting your lifestyle creep on hold.

What does that mean? It means deciding how much you need to live on, and as your income rises *above* that, don't allow your lifestyle to creep up by the same amount. That doesn't mean you can't prosper financially, just don't continue to consume greater amounts. When it's time to give yourself a raise, commit to only absorbing half of it into your personal budget and saving or investing the rest. That way, every increase in spending is offset by an increase in savings.

The message here isn't to live in poverty. It's to live within your means. If you want more, then you need to increase your means first. And remember: as long as your personal budget is unbalanced, your practice budget will be too. And that'll mean spending more and more time seeing clients until it gets past the point that's healthy for anyone.

Strategy #3: Review expenses regularly and set budgets

Just as your personal expenses can easily creep upward and consume all your income, so too can the costs of running your practice.

Every year, take the time to:

- Review the expenses of running your business.
- Identify the large expense areas and look for ways to reduce them.
- Set annual budgets for marketing, improvements, staffing, et cetera. Yes, you may have to adapt these through the year, but without limits, you'll find yourself constantly surprised—and unprepared.

Naturally, to do all this, you'll need to know how much you're actually spending. And that requires bookkeeping. If you don't have good monthly, quarterly, and yearly accounting information, you're going to need it. You can do it yourself if you're good at it and you enjoy it, or you can pay someone else. Just make sure you have it. No information means no control, and no control puts you on the slippery slope to Burnout.

Strategy #4: Use debt wisely

Does being financially wise mean you can't invest in your practice using borrowed money? Of course not. It can be very challenging to do some things without debt. Can you imagine saving enough money to buy a home in *cash*? While some people do, it's tough for most.

Here are a few tips for using debt wisely in your practice:

Don't borrow for expenses

Borrow money for *investments* that will help you grow your practice, like new tools, equipment, and office improvements. To help tell the difference, ask yourself this question: *Will this help grow my practice continuously, or is it a one-time expense?* If it's the latter, then it's best not to go down that route. Emergencies happen, but be aware of what it is you're taking on debt for.

Find friendly debt first

Family members and other contacts can be better sources of money than credit cards. The terms are usually good—and negotiable. Banks are fine, but generally not as flexible. Don't settle for the quickest, easiest debt if it comes with a big long-term price tag in the form of inflexibility or high interest.

Calculate the return

If you buy a new piece of equipment, for example, how long will it take to get back the money you've invested? If you need to use it 150 times to pay for itself, how long will that take? Some things, like office improvements, are difficult to calculate a return on. Just remember: the harder it is to calculate the return, the more critically you should examine whether or not you *really* need to buy it.

Strategy #5: Pay yourself first

Get in the habit of paying yourself consistently. It's far too easy for your practice to consume all the cash flow and for you to find yourself still breaking even five years down the road. Just look at how easy it is to spend all the money in your personal bank account. As we've seen, your personal expenses have a habit of rising to meet the available cash, and your practice is no different.

It doesn't matter how much you pay yourself. Ten dollars a month is fine. But what's important is to start the habit. Just set up an automated system and forget about it. Everyone in practice can afford ten bucks, and believe us, simply getting started will make a difference.

And don't forget to give yourself regular raises. Stretch yourself. Pay a tiny bit past what you can afford, and you'll find your practice will adjust to accommodate the increased expense.

Along with paying yourself comes paying your *future* self. In 1926, George Clason wrote *The Wealthiest Man in Babylon,* a parable about a man seeking the secrets to wealth in ancient times. Its most powerful secret—saving ten percent of your earnings—is the cornerstone of almost all of today's financial planning. The challenge is that most people wait too long to start.

Take ten percent of whatever salary you pay yourself and sock it aside. This is your wealth fund that you never touch. Set up the process at your bank so that the funds are transferred out automatically and forget about it. Don't worry if you're just saving one dollar out of your ten-dollar salary right now. Just stick with it and you'll be surprised at how quickly it adds up.

Strategy #6: Decide what "enough" is

Financial balance doesn't mean finding a level of income or wealth that you can "live with" and staying that way forever. That is a legitimate choice, but it's not your only option. The steps above are designed to allow you to continue to grow your financial wealth gradually without sacrificing your time, health, and relationships.

More than ever, we're faced with conflicting advice and philosophies surrounding wealth. The bible says, "Money is the root of all evil," yet the abundance gurus of our age tell us that wealth is natural, good, and healthy. Where does the truth lie?

The truth is that *there isn't a truth.* You can do much good with money, for yourself and for others. But you can also do much damage. What is undeniable is that how you generate wealth, and how you use it, is a choice.

Choose wisely.

Each of these strategies for taking control of money is a decision that describes the precise boundaries of the finances in your life. "I don't spend more than this amount," or "I always pay myself first," are lines in the sand that successful practitioners don't cross lightly. Yes, you could continue to spend everything in your personal and business accounts, but that's the equivalent of brushing away all the lines in the sand (and with them, your chances of balancing both your finances and your time).

Inherent in financial balance is the idea that your practice has to do more than just generate revenue. It has to make a *profit*. After you pay the bills, there needs to be something left over or your practice will be gradually digging itself deeper and deeper into a hole. Profit comes from growing your practice using the strategies from the previous chapters, but it also comes from understanding how money flows *out* of your practice, too, and drawing lines in the sand accordingly.

You need to play good financial offense by helping clients across the river and leveraging them, but you also need to play good defense, too. Finding financial balance isn't about choosing poverty. It's simply about not fooling yourself and not allowing financial deception to spread through your entire life, slowly decaying your relationships, your passion for your work, and your health.

THE THIRD LINE IN THE SAND: HEALER BALANCE

You'd think that a healthy schedule and a solid financial footing would make just about anyone happy and balanced, and to a large extent that's true. Taking control of your time and money will make an enormous difference in the level of stress you feel and your ability to enjoy your work *and* non-work time.

Health care practitioners, though, are faced with balance challenges that go beyond those of the average overworked citizen. Practitioners tend to bring their work home with them more so than those in other professions. They often find themselves riding the cresting and breaking waves of client success.

They feel elation when clients do well, and discomfort or even depression when they don't. It can be a vicious roller coaster. Even practitioners with great time balance and a solid income can find their way to Burnout.

Ayala Pines, author of *Career Burnout: Causes and Cures*, states that job burnout comes not from long hours, but from not having an impact at work. In her research, nurses in pediatric burn units had the highest burnout rate not because of long hours, but simply because *they were unable to alleviate the pain*.

"Just don't bring your work home with you," is a sentiment that's far too easy to say and far too difficult to put into action. Over time, many practitioners learn to place distance between themselves and their clients, but that comes at a certain cost, too. Some professions rely on that connection, and there are levels of detachment that just aren't possible.

Over a long career, not all of your clients are going to get better. Some are going to get worse. Some will die. Intellectually, you know that you won't be able to help everyone. But at an emotional level, how do we keep the valley from turning into Burnout in disguise?

If your level of success with clients is going to have an impact on your balance, then the best strategy for coping with an inability to help is to *redefine what success means*.

1. Define practitioner success

We tend to equate "success" with "cured." If you consider every "uncured" client as a failure, or if you consider complete condition resolution as the only form of success, you'll soon find your way to Burnout no matter how much money you're generating.

There is one clear distinction you can make in your approach to clients that can radically improve your success rate: **define success for you, the practitioner, as moving your clients to the next step in their healing—whatever that step may be.**

What does that mean? First of all, we're acknowledging that healing is a process. For some clients and conditions, it's a short process. For others, it may be a long and winding road with many detours. By acknowledging this process, you are accepting that there may be more than one stop on the road and that success does *not* necessarily mean cured. And even if it does, it doesn't have to mean cured by *you*.

Your role may be large or it may be small. But in every case, your role is to move the client *forward* in the process. You may well reach the end goal with every client, but what's most important is that you move them to the next step.

What might that step be? It could be simply relieving their complaint, but it could also be helping them prepare to die. Perhaps it's referring them elsewhere, or it might even mean discharging them from your practice when you can no longer help. The next step in their process can take many different forms. If you only accept "cured" as a successful outcome, then your professional life may be a short one.

In our clinic, our simple mission is to help people feel better. The real power of that aim, though, is that even when we can't help clinically, we can still help them feel better. Even when our clients have terminal illnesses, we can *still* help them feel better in some way.

Success doesn't mean cured. Your job is to move your clients to the next step. It's all you can do, but you can do it in an exceptional manner and feel great about it. If you struggle to create and maintain boundaries between the health of your clients and your own life, try to redefine what success as a practitioner really means. Does establishing boundaries between them and you mean that you've failed to connect to or empathize with clients? No. But it does mean that their problems are not yours. Keep in mind that getting them to the next step in their healing is your primary goal.

2. Define client success

If practitioner success means moving your client to the next step, then we need to know what that next step *is*. One of the greatest things you can do for your practice and your clients is to clearly define the road ahead. It's great for business, as we saw from using the first lever to get clients to return to your practice, but it's also indispensible for ensuring that everyone involved has a clear understanding of what the next step on the journey is.

You can define that next step using the following questions:

Client Outcomes

- What are the client's physical and/or emotional objectives?
- Is what the client's trying to achieve realistic?
- How will the client measure progress toward those goals?
- How will you, the practitioner, know when these objectives have been met?
- How will the client measure success?

Treatment Timelines

- How long will it take?
- How often will the client visit you?
- At what point will you re-evaluate the plan?
- What level of ongoing visits (if any) will be required?

Practitioner and Client Responsibilities

- What are the contributions of the practitioner and of the client?
- What happens if one (or both) of you fail to meet your responsibilities?

Something remarkable happens when both you *and* your clients know the answers to these questions: *everything works.* Your job becomes easier. Clients move further in their healing. And even if they don't, they still feel better about their relationship with you. We have clients who we've never been able to help in a clinical sense but who still refer to us regularly because of this clarity.

REDRAWING LINES: BALANCE AND REBALANCE

You can draw your lines in the sand anywhere. They're different for every practitioner. What's important is to draw them—to actually create the boundaries. A practice without them will eventually spin out of balance in some way.

At their core, the lines in the sand are about "artificial scarcity." Rather than simply giving your practice *all* of your time until there is no more, for example, we draw a line and say, "This is all there is to give." Yes, technically there *is* other time. But you need that time for other things like your health and your relationships.

In the same way that having money withdrawn automatically from a bank account is an effective way for most people to pay themselves first and build long-term savings, limiting your practice hours is an effective way of paying yourself first in *time*, too.

Limiting what hours we give to our practices ensures that we don't spend more time than we should. Limiting what we leave in our bank accounts ensures that we don't spend more money than we should. It's not limiting how abundant you are—it's simply taking control of how that abundance is allocated.

But does that mean we're forever restricted by these self-imposed borders? That we can never stretch out to help someone in need outside of our boundaries? That we can never take a financial risk? Absolutely not.

If you've ever watched a gymnast or a circus performer, you've seen the astounding feats of balance and control that they're capable of. And while they seem to have the ability to remain perfectly immobile and still, what's really happening is quite different. Physical balance—even the act of standing still—is an incredibly complex dance of sensory inputs, body signals, and fine muscle movements.

Balance in your practice is surprisingly similar. It's a moving target. As your life changes and as your practice changes, you'll find that staying balanced in your life is not much different from staying balanced on a tightrope. It's a constant process of assessment, adjustment, and reassessment.

Like your body's physical balance, though, you can make work-life balance a relatively unconscious activity if you set your vision clearly enough. All your initial big-picture work of defining your practice, your clients, and your work schedule, as well as managing your money, will pay off in a comfortable, healthy balance that's easier to maintain. Balance is not about making every day the same as the last, or being afraid to commit resources to something new. The secret is to examine the impact of changes on your balance *before* you commit.

The sand line isn't a wall. It's not a barricade. Anyone can step across a line in the sand. Staying in balance isn't about creating an impenetrable barrier. It's a matter of carefully defining what comes in and out of that circle, and for how long. It's about looking down at the line in the sand at your feet and asking, "Do I really want to cross this?"

There will be times when temptation rears its head. Increased client loads. A side opportunity. New personal demands. There will be times when you choose to do more—to help people by stepping across the line. Times when you might step over the time line, or the money line, by working too much or spending too much. It happens to all of us.

You may even decide over time to move your line. That's the beauty of sand lines—they're not written in stone. In fact, they have a way of gradually vanishing in the winds that blow down the path. A new baby, a new relationship, a turning point in your career, a sabbatical, or any other life change is cause for reexamining the line.

The trick is to *have* the line to begin with. To be able to look back and see that you crossed it, and to use the line as a benchmark for moving back into balance.

While sacrifice is not bad—and in some cases can be essential—it's important to make the *right* sacrifices. Changes have a way of becoming habits, and habits have a sticking power that's tough to break. **The challenge of the valley is to not trade your health for the health of your clients.**

If this really is a journey, then in order to count the steps it takes to reach Success, *we first have to last long enough to get there.* That means finding a way to pace ourselves for the long run of our careers without burning out on the sprints.

Like the valley in our story, the valley of private practice is familiar, comfortable, and really quite beautiful. In short, it's a nice place to be. And if you can draw clear lines in the valley, then you'll be able to protect the things that are most important to you.

Draw your lines and keep the sacred as sacred. It really does work.

But the story doesn't end here. There's another challenge awaiting us in the valley, one that goes beyond battling external forces that threaten your balance.

To understand it, we need to head back to the path one more time.

9. The Long Lever

The obstacle is the path.

~Zen proverb

*L*ife is good.

That could be your motto now that you've created a life in the valley. Several years have passed since your arrival, and now, surrounded by the natural beauty of the high canyon walls and blessed with an abundance of clients arriving daily at your doorstep, you've settled into a comfortable routine. Life is indeed good.

Of course, it's taken some time to master the lines in the sand. At first people never noticed your lines, or occasional changes in the weather would wipe them out and you'd need to diligently redefine your boundaries and reclaim your personal space. But after a while it became a habit, and you realize now that when you're in balance, you're able to help others more effectively than ever.

Yes, life is good.

Well. It's *pretty* good. Lately there have been so many people who need your help that you're forced to make them wait. Some of them do wait, which is an inconvenience to them, but what really bothers you is when people *don't* wait. They drift away from the valley and you wonder what happens to them. Do they ever get the help they need?

Other times, when you know they really *can't* wait, you're forced to make more and more exceptions to your carefully drawn boundaries. Your time is being stretched thinner and thinner. The late afternoons you used to spend watching the sun set at the end of the valley are now spent helping others. It's still rewarding, but you're stretched so thinly now that you simply don't have the time to help the way you once did. You're beginning to feel like you're not doing your vision of Success justice.

But you also realize that there's more to this feeling than simply not being able to help everyone in the way you want. If you're completely honest with yourself, you realize that the routine has become a little stale. And lurking just below the level of your consciousness is an idea that you've been reluctant to acknowledge: *what if this is all there is?*

Lately, you've found your thoughts drifting to the rockslide blocking the end of the valley. At first it seemed like a blessing—a shelter that protected the beauty of this place. But lately you've been sneaking little peeks at it. And occasionally you find yourself beginning to wonder if the rockslide is protecting you or *trapping* you. As the days pass, you find yourself looking for excuses to wander closer to the end of the valley, wondering again what might be on the other side.

One day, as you pick your way along the edge of the rock pile, you see a flat piece of wood protruding from the strewn rubble. You kick away the stones and earth, and with some digging and yanking, you finally pull it free.

It's a broken signpost. In the fading light you can see a painted arrow, and just below it is one faint word: *Success.*

Your first thought is that the sign must have been pointing back into the valley for practitioners entering from the other side.

But then it hits you. *Maybe it was pointing onward!* Are you already at Success, like you've thought all along, or is it actually on the other side of the rockslide? Your thoughts drift back to the very first day of your journey, to the words left for you at the beginning of the trail: *follow the path to its end.*

Your stomach churns in a mixture of fear and excitement. *What if this isn't the end?*

As you gaze at the enormous rockslide, you realize that there's no way to know without climbing over.

But how do you reach the other side? The landslide is *massive*. Given enough time, and with enough help, you know you could eventually scale it. But where are you going to get the time and resources to do that? And what about all those people back—

Your thoughts are interrupted by the sound of voices behind you. It seems that you're needed in the valley again.

With a sigh, you turn away from the rocks—and your thoughts—and head back to work.

We ran into Angela at a conference. She was running a busy practice filled with great clients. She had a waiting list and was making a living doing what she'd always wanted to do. Life was good.

"I think in another ten or 15 years, I'll be in a spot where I can retire. I can sell the practice, and do something different," she said.

It sounded like everything was working out just great. In an industry where many struggle, she was a busy practitioner.

"There's just one problem," she said. "I don't think I can make it that long."

Angela had done everything right. She'd started a practice, provided great care, and used some thoughtful and effective marketing to grow her client base. The problem was that she was headed toward Burnout.

After 15 years of practice, she was tired. She took vacations, and balanced her schedule, but most of the year she worked full time seeing clients. Now, she was faced with another decade or two of the same thing.

And naturally, she was hoping to earn a little more over those next ten or twenty years. The trouble was that she'd reached the healthy limit of the amount of time she could work. Adding more hours to the schedule wasn't a realistic option, but that was the only way she could see to really increase her income by any reasonable amount.

Even with careful boundaries around her time and money, she was at the end of her growth. The next decade or two looked very similar and, perhaps more ominous still, the road ahead felt less *inspiring* than it ever had before.

Angela was trapped in the valley.

Contrast Angela's experience, though, with that of Sarah Aldrich, a pilates instructor in New Haven, Connecticut. Early on, Sarah realized that there were limits to what she could do. "As a pilates instructor," she said, "my body is my business. If I teach 35 hours per week, my head will explode."

Sarah started her practice in 2009. Within a year of opening her doors, her practice was busy and growing quickly. The difference, however, was that Sarah was working less and less, teaching only in the mornings and focusing on growing her business and staying balanced during the rest of her day. Unlike Angela, Sarah's time had become more flexible as her practice grew, not less. And her income was poised to rise further still.

Sarah had done something different. She'd somehow created a way to leave the valley when she chose. To understand what Sarah did, though, we first need to have a closer look at Angela's dilemma.

Like many practitioners, Angela had discovered that after some time spent basking in the valley, any (or all) of the following began to happen:

You want more

As a culture we have a tendency to adapt quite readily to higher levels of income and greater levels of achievement. Regardless of whether it's good or not, it's *true*. It happens to most practitioners, and it's likely to show up in your life as well.

You become restless

It may be hard to believe early on in your practice, but the day may come when you become a little bored. You might want to return to school, take some time off, or even completely change your current profession.

Your life changes

A new baby arrives on the scene. Or you get sick. Or you need to care for a loved one. Perhaps you discover a new passion that demands more of your time. These are all twists in the ever-changing game of life, and you can expect one in your life, too.

You want to help more

Even if you don't want more money, more time, or something new in your life, and even if you never lose your passion for your current practice, what happens when your current practice is simply *full*? If you keep growing, there will come a day when you'll have to do the one thing you never trained for: you'll have to say "no" to someone you know you can help.

What Angela was also discovering was what Sarah already knew: she couldn't solve her dilemma by simply working *more*. You can't help more, earn more, learn more, or have more if doing those things requires time you just don't have. Angela was learning what every practitioner realizes after some time in the valley: **the limits of your time in solo practice are also the limits of your growth.**

So what's the solution? What did Sarah do that Angela hasn't? If the path to Success is going to eventually lead us to become overworked and under-satisfied, how do we move ahead? The solution lies in the difference between how Sarah and Angela approached the challenge of life in the valley.

Angela is still stuck. She's in solo practice, struggling to grow without burning out. Sarah's chosen a different route. As soon as her practice became profitable—about six months in—she began looking for another pilates instructor to teach some of her classes. That created the freedom she needed to continue to work on her business and keep her life in balance. The reason why Sarah's only working half of Angela's schedule is that *she's no longer alone.* She's drawn her lines in the sand, yes, but she's also chosen to leave the valley by transforming her practice into a *business.*

To understand what leaving the valley means, we need to have a closer look at the difference between a *practice* and a *business*. Until now, we've tossed the terms around indiscriminately (as most practitioners do if you ask), but it's time to get more specific in our definitions.

There is one simple question that will determine right now if you have a practice or a business:

> *Does your practice make money when you're not there?*

That is, when you leave the office (to go on vacation, take a sick day, or spend some quality time with your friends or family) does revenue continue to flow, or does it stop dead?

If you prefer not to look at the question through the lens of money, try rephrasing it this way:

> *Does your practice help people when you're not there?*

That is, when you leave the office do people continue to get care for their health concerns? If the money and the helping stop when you stop, then chances are you have a practice, not a business.

Let's be clear: there's nothing wrong with that. As a matter of fact, that's how most of the world works. They get paid for their time. And you, too, can have a long, successful career as a CAM professional simply by selling yours. The challenge is that it can be tough to juggle money, time, health, and relationships as a solo practitioner. Sooner or later you're going to find that, like Angela, you want more time, more money, or more of both, and a standard solo practice is unlikely to give you that. **If you want to escape the treadmill of trading time for money, you need to move beyond solo practice.**

That means leaving the valley. It means getting past the mother of all boulders—that huge rockslide that's blocking your way.

In your practice, the rockslide is made up of things like the fear of change and the risk of the unknown. The feeling that we don't have enough time to make changes. The uncertainty about how to take what we've created from practice to business. Each fear, each uncertainty, is another rock in the landslide—just one more piece of rubble to get past before moving closer to Success. Just as the river is uncertainty for your clients, the rockslide is uncertainty for you. Who will take care of your clients while you're busy trying to scale your way to Success? What if you fall, or worse yet, get crushed?

Getting past that rockslide starts with wrapping your mind around why leaving the valley is worth the effort.

The benefits of business

Leaving the valley and transitioning from solo practice offers a multitude of benefits. Some are more obvious than others, but each is a compelling reason in its own right to at least consider the possibility of leaving the valley.

Money

As a health care practitioner, you sell your time. A 30-minute appointment costs this much, and a 15-minute treatment costs that much. It's a pretty simple formula—for example, you give an hour of your time and your customer gives you $150. This system is easy to implement and easy to track, but it limits your earnings. After all, you've only got 24 hours in a day and you can't sell them all. Everybody's got to sleep.

Transforming from practice to business can help you find that extra financial reward without selling more time. It allows revenue to flow into your business in a way that's not directly tied to you seeing clients. No, money's not the pinnacle of Success. But in this world, you need at least some of it to stay afloat.

If you're still not convinced, ask yourself this: *how much stress are you experiencing in your life because of a lack of money?*

Balance

Why did you become a CAM practitioner? Did you want to help people? Make a decent living? Maybe have control over your life and schedule? Travel? Be free of financial stress? Be your own boss? Retire early? Retire wealthy?

Most CAM professionals are interested in all of those things. But if you speak to them, you'll find that only a handful have found the "sweet spot" that balances their need for income with their desire to help people *and* lead a balanced life themselves. Most are either overworked, or cash strapped, or worse still, a combination of both.

So what's wrong with just running a practice? The answer, still, is nothing—provided that you don't need any extra money, time, balance, or joy in your life beyond what a solo practice provides. In this day and age, simply running your practice like an old-fashioned family doctor is a long-term plan to eliminate freedom from your life and replace it with stress and financial worry.

Future value

One of the nice thoughts about turning your practice into a business is the idea that you're building something of value that you can sell. You don't *have* to sell it—in fact, if you make the transformation successfully, there may be no need to—but it's nice to know that if life throws you a curve, or if you want to move on to other things, you can sell your business.

A business is worth more than a practice. Here's why:

- A business can simply generate more profit than a solo practice.
- A business has much greater growth potential—for a new owner, the sky's the limit.
- A business that generates revenue in the absence of its owner is more attractive than one that requires the owner to be there.
- A business that doesn't require an owner to be present all the time can be sold to *anyone*. A solo practice oper- ated by a chiropractor, for example, can really only be sold to another chiropractor who can fill the solo-

owner's shoes. After all, in solo practice, the owner is the practitioner, too.

Transitioning from a practice to a business offers you the opportunity, in essence, to pay yourself *twice*. Once for your work as a practitioner, and again for your work as a business owner.

Safety net

Hiring people, owning things, managing things, perhaps increasing your costs—at first glance it can seem like growing from a practice to a business increases your risk. While that may be true in some ways, *not* running a true business carries its own risks.

In a solo practice you've got all your eggs in one basket. If something happens to you, the money stops. Just like that. Being insured can help, but that can cost you, which means you need to work more hours, which... well, you know where that leads.

Solo practice balances your entire career and economic future on one point: *you*. That's not only risky, but it's also a lot of pressure. A health care business mitigates that risk by offering you other sources of income besides selling your time for money.

Flexibility

Ever wanted to take a day or a week off to do something special, but you felt you couldn't? In a practice, every vacation you take costs a fortune—the cost of the trip *plus* all the money you *didn't* earn while you were away. A business allows you to earn when you're not working. Like the safety net, a business gives you choices. It lets you take time off to pursue other interests. Want to have a baby? Take some maternity or paternity leave? Travel? Volunteer in another country? Go on a field trip with your kid's class? These things become a lot easier if your practice generates some cash in your absence.

Continued growth

You can only grow so much in a solo practice. Some specialized services or treatments require a critical mass of clients to be viable. If you've ever wanted to have more office space, or specialize in a certain treatment, then you may need to grow to a certain size to do it. And that size may be one you can't reach on your own, or one that simply takes too *long* to reach on your own. A business can give you the size you need sooner rather than later.

Greater reach

The solo practice model limits how many people you can help. For the practitioner who got into the profession out of an intrinsic need to help others, this can be unsettling at a deep, emotional level. Many practitioners are simply unable to accept this truth, but can't bring themselves to turn away new clients. They're the CAM doctors who find themselves in Burnout.

Transitioning to a business allows you to continue to help for as long as you like.

Collaboration

By far the most common complaint we hear from CAM practitioners is that they feel alone. Huge numbers of practitioners are in solo practices or in clinics where they have no reason or opportunity to truly collaborate with others. It's a lonely job. Shifting from a practice to a business, as we'll see, can change the loneliness of solo practice into something far more collaborative.

THE LONG LEVER: HOW TO LEAVE THE VALLEY

This chapter is about leaving the valley by transforming from a solo health care practice to a health care *business*. It's about reaching more people and continuing to grow beyond the limits of what you can do alone. It's also about creating a legacy by helping people even when the road to Success lasts longer than your time as a practitioner.

There are all kinds of businesses out there—an infinite number of variations in the old formula of trading goods or services for money. And for each kind, there are successes and failures.

Within this huge pool of business possibilities are many variations that are related to what you do now. Regardless of your modality, you can use your experience to start any number of ventures that meet our criteria for "making money when you're not there." You might write a book or rent space in your office to someone else. You could start a website that dispenses products or information about your particular area of expertise. You could become a reseller of supplement products or join any number of network marketing organizations that might be a fit for a health care provider. The possibilities are endless.

What we're going to focus on here, however, is very specific: taking your current *job*, which is as a provider of health care services, and turning that same job into a *business* that can help more people and generate more revenue than it can in its current form.

Remember the levers that let you shift those boulders that were blocking the path to Success! Those levers let you do more in your practice with less. This chapter is really about another lever—the longest lever of all. One that can take you to another level that can't be achieved when you're flying solo.

That lever is having *other* people do the work of treating clients. The reason we don't lump it in with the rest of the levers is that the shifts in thinking required to move from practice to business are very, very different from simply growing your practice as a solo practitioner. To make the leap from practice to business—or from practitioner to entrepreneur—you need to do more than change your practice. You need to change your *mind*.

At this point, if you think that running a business is not for you, try to keep an open mind for a little longer. The shift from healer to entrepreneur can be slow and subtle, or dramatic and rapid. You might make the shift over a day, over a decade, or never. But you won't lose anything by sticking with us for a few more pages.

To leave the valley, you'll need help. But this time, you'll need more than just the support of your clients. To put the time and energy into climbing out of the valley and onward to Success you'll need people who can stay in the valley and help clients while you do the work of climbing. To leave the valley, you're going to need more people on your team *who deliver health care.*

Why people make the difference

We know now that your practice is, for the most part, a service business, and that the amount of *serving* you can do is limited by... well, *you*. You might argue that if you sell supplements, for example, you've already made the transition from practice to business since those sales can happen when you're not there. That may be true to a limited extent, but even then, you need to continue to work with the clients who will, in turn, buy the products. Once you stop serving people, those product sales will eventually slow down, too.

In order to meet our definition of "making money when you're not there" (remember, that also means "helping people heal when you're not there," too), we're going to need more than just some extra products. Yes, adding products to your practice is the second lever at work, but it's not going to help you reach more people when you've got your back to the valley wall. To do that, you're going to need other *practitioners.*

There are very few one-person businesses in the world that can grow and make money without their owners being present. In an industry like health care, which is for the most part service-based, it's even less likely. On the other hand, there are many thousands of multi-person businesses that provide important products and services—and generate revenue—without their owners being there. If you want to help more clients *and* stay balanced, then you're going to need more people in your business.

Skip Van Meter, LAc, co-founder of *Working Class Acupuncture*, stresses that to succeed in the long term, you'll to need grow and add people to your practice:

> *"That long-term thing: making a living so that I have a lifestyle I like, so that my kids can go to college, so that I can retire sometime etc.: I'm afraid it can't really be*

> *done with just a solo practice, CA [community acu-*
> *puncture] or BA [boutique acupuncture]. I need to*
> *work with a bunch of other people for it to happen.*
>   *"...one can only go so far in a solo practice and ...*
> *regardless of if you are doing a CA or BA clinic, work-*
> *ing by yourself will burn you out eventually. You need*
> *support from others and you need to be responsible to*
> *others in order to succeed—and by others I mean co-*
> *workers, not clients."[9]*

Solo practice has a limit—the amount you're willing to work. To break free of that restriction, you'll need other people to do what you do (and more). This lever—the longest one of them all—is used for shifting the boulders at the end of the canyon. In real terms, what this lever represents is more people. And not just administrative and support staff, but honest-to-goodness practitioners who deliver care.

For most practitioners, though, this idea of adding more people to the mix is a scary prospect. It carries with it the idea of hemorrhaging cash flow, personality conflicts, and extra paperwork. In essence, moving beyond a single practitioner operation seems risky and expensive. It seems like longer hours and more work. It seems *harder*.

But it doesn't have to be. If done properly, it will make you more financially successful, give you more balance, and provide *more* cash flow, not less. Here's how you can find the right people to help you leave the valley:

Leaving the valley, step #1: Choose the right professional

Remember, this isn't about front desk staff, admin support, receptionists, website consultants, bookkeepers, or accountants. Those frontline and behind-the-scenes support staff are critically important, and without question you'll need more of them as you grow. What we're going to focus on here, though, is *adding more people who deliver care to your clients*. Those are the people who generate revenue in a practice, and so it's more of them that we need to help you transition out of the valley.

But who are those people? If you're a TCM practitioner or a chiropractor, who do you need to add to your practice? If you're a busy bodyworker or a nutritionist, who should you seek out to help you continue to grow and continue to reach more people? To better understand who those people are (and when and why you might want them), we're going to break them into three types of care providers: *duplicators*, *diversifiers*, and *technicians*.

Duplicators

In a nutshell, "duplicators" do what you do with clients. If you're a nutritionist who works with clients to define and refine their diets, then your duplicator is another nutritionist (or equivalent) who can do that same job. If you're a chiropractor, your duplicator is another chiropractor who can treat clients. Your duplicator performs the exact same technical health care procedures and processes you do.

Diversifiers

"Diversifiers," on the other hand, bring something different to the mix. If our chiropractor from the previous example adds a nutritionist to his business, then that nutritionist is a diversifier. If a homeopath brings a reiki practitioner into her business, then that reiki practitioner is a diversifier.

Technicians

"Technicians" are a subset of duplicators. They perform *part* of the duties that a practitioner does (usually the parts that require less skill or training and fewer credentials). When you see the dental assistant or hygienist to have your teeth cleaned, you're seeing a technician. When a naturopath hires an assistant to take lab samples or do diagnostic testing, she's hired a technician to take over *billable work* that she normally does herself.

It may seem like a subtle difference, but duplicating and diversifying in particular are distinctly different tactics for adding more people to your business. So how do you know who to add and when to add them?

Adding duplicators

Remember Sue Painter? She's the massage therapist who booked her practice solid a year in advance. She's been a busy therapist for many years. Last year, however, she moved into a larger office space with four treatment rooms. She now has three other massage therapists working for her, as well as a receptionist/office manager. "I just can't work at the level I used to 13 years ago," she said. Now, her staff takes the bulk of her client load.

Sue's strategy was to duplicate, and as you might expect, it's a very common approach. One of the very first ways that CAM professionals begin to make the transformation from a practice to a business is to try to clone themselves. The chiropractor brings on an associate DC and takes a percentage of his billings The massage therapist rents a room to another massage therapist to offset the fixed costs of her office.

The great advantage of duplicating is that it's familiar, and for most people, "familiar" means "easier." If you're an acupuncturist, you already understand the needs of other acupuncturists and the needs of acupuncture clients. Plus, you've already got the clients. That makes bringing another practitioner into the office simpler: you use the same equipment, the same space, the same billing software, and similar client processes.

Bringing another similar practitioner into your business also brings camaraderie and collaboration. Most CAM practices are solo gigs, and working alone can wear you out. Many practitioners find themselves relieved when they can actually take a vacation without worrying that there's no one in the office to deal with acute issues and emergencies in their absence.

The strength of duplication, though, is also its weakness: duplicators do what you do, and no matter how you slice it, keeping two identical practitioners busy generally requires twice as many clients. Adding an associate to your business doesn't necessarily help its growth. When you add someone who does the same thing as you do to the mix, you create two mouths to feed instead of one, and that doesn't help anyone unless you've got more food than you can stomach. That's the most important distinction of duplicators—*they tend to divide your client base rather than expand it.*

Nonetheless, at some point a busy practitioner needs help. You'll know you're ready to duplicate when you fit any or all of the following:

- You're so busy that you'll happily refer new and existing clients to a new practitioner in your space. In fact, you can't *wait* to find someone so you can start offloading clients.
- You've got a waiting list. If you're actively turning people away or making them wait, then you're in a good position to start duplicating.
- You want to work less—even if it means cutting income—and you want to shift your current clients to someone new.
- You want to transition out of seeing clients in order to simply grow and manage your business.

Each of these criteria has one thing in common: to duplicate effectively, you need to be willing to give up clients to someone else.

You've probably noticed, however, that many practitioners do the opposite. They desperately seek out someone—usually an associate—to join their practice because they're *not* busy and they need help covering costs. We'll look at the strengths and weaknesses of the associate model later. For now, let's look at diversifiers—those professionals who bring something *different* into the mix.

Adding diversifiers

As a solo practitioner, you can only personally diversify so much. You can only learn, master, and practice so many techniques, modalities, or treatments. So, to diversify to any extent in your practice, you'll require the skills of someone else.

Diversity offers a number of advantages that simply adding another one of *you* does not.

First of all, it expands your client base. If you're a chiropractor and you add a naturopath to your office, you may be opening your doors to a whole new group of customers who aren't interested in what you're currently offering but are interested in what you're *adding*. Instead of bringing on another chiropractor and potentially fighting over the same slice of the pie, why not expand the niche of people who you're appealing to?

Second, diversity draws more revenue from your current client base. Clients coming in for that chiropractic adjustment might also like a massage, some acupuncture, or any number of other possible treatments. So, simply put, a client might now spend twice as much in your office. That extra revenue is money you might never have received otherwise, despite having that client in your office regularly. Diversifying puts that second lever to work by getting your clients to spend more of their dollars in your office.

Unlike duplicating, diversifying is something you can do at any time, no matter how many clients you have. Because you're adding something new that your clients can use, you don't run into the same challenges that you'd face by adding a copy of yourself. It's another strategy Sue Painter employed when she collocated with an esthetician, enabling her clients to bring more revenue into her clinic. Naturopath Aranka Jones added her esthetician the day she opened her doors; the diversification provided an entry point for esthetics customers to consider naturopathy, delivered revenue that she might not have received otherwise, and did it all whether she was there or not. Her diversifier also did double-duty, serving as a receptionist too.

Aranka diversified from day one. Sue diversified after being in practice for over a decade. And you? Here are some signs that it may be time to diversify your practice:

- You want to start transitioning from practice to business now, but your current client base isn't big enough to add another identical practitioner (a duplicator) without cannibalizing your own revenue.
- Your clients are continually asking for a related service that you don't offer.
- You see a gap in the current marketplace that isn't being filled. For example, there might be a shortage of nutritionists in your area.
- Your profession (or the marketplace) is shifting in a way that's going to make it harder for you to continue to grow your practice. Diversity lowers your risk. It gives you other sources of income in case the revenues from your modality dry up for one reason or another. As laws, popular trends, and economic realities shift, so do the ways in which cash flows into your practice. Diversifying helps reduce the risk of those shifts.
- You have a large client base that can start to use a new offering right away.

There are drawbacks to diversifiers, too. The greatest of these is that a new profession or modality also means dealing in something unfamiliar. You may be an expert in your own field and have an excellent understanding of your clients and your local market, but can you say the same of a different profession? Diversifiers require a little more homework. You'll need to go beyond, "Whoa! I'm really busy! I'll have to hire someone like me pronto," and really dig into whether or not a different offering will fit with your vision, your difference, and your existing and future clients.

Adding technicians

Michael Gerber, author of *The E-Myth*, uses the term "technician" to describe the people who do the technical work of a business. Dentists, for example, don't hire other dentists to clean teeth. They hire dental hygienists. Even though another dentist could do the job, they'll choose a hygienist because they're qualified, they're cheaper, and they have great skills gained from focusing on one specific niche.

The same applies to CAM professions. Physical therapists may be able to hire athletic therapists or kinesiologists to do some of their treatments. A busy acupuncturist might hire a technician to remove needles.

Unlike duplicators and diversifiers, technicians are resources that many professionals can add from day one. Technicians do *parts* of the job you currently do—ideally, they focus on something that requires less skill, training, or credentials.

Handing over some of your current practitioner responsibilities to a technician serves several purposes:

- It frees up some of your time, which you can use to work on your business, see more clients, or pursue other interests.
- It keeps you focused on the higher-skill areas of your profession (or your "core genius," as we like to think of it).
- It makes your practice more profitable. If you can pay a technician far less to do the lower-skill parts of your work, then you can focus on the higher-paying portion. It's similar to having a receptionist deal with the administrative parts of your job—those tasks just don't require the same skill set and credentials.

As long as there are aspects of your work that can be done by someone less skilled, adding technicians is something that can happen at almost any time in your business. You don't need to wait until your practice is booked solid. In fact, adding a technician is often an easier interim step than adding your first duplicator. When a physiotherapist has a kinesiologist or athletic therapist carry out his treatment plans, for example, he can more comfortably hire another physiotherapist knowing that his duplicator will be focused on high revenue-generating, highly skilled activities.

Leaving the valley, step #2: Choose the right relationship

Duplicating and diversifying are both very common. They offer the twin benefits of providing easy, inexpensive practice startup for new practitioners, as well as extra cash flow and freedom for more established ones. The idea of having other people treat your clients isn't new, and it's not rocket science. What can be challenging, though, is doing it in a way that *works*.

Once you've chosen the right professionals, you need to decide what their relationship with your clinic will be. Are they associates? Employees? Contractors? There are four common relationships between CAM business owners and the other professionals who work with them. Each has its own strengths and weaknesses:

Associate (fee split)

Associate arrangements are the most common ways to add more practitioners to a practice. Remember the example of our chiropractor seeking more cash flow and relief from monthly overhead? To make it easy, she hires another chiropractor on a fee split. That way, the associate DC costs her nothing when he's not seeing clients. This approach is very low-risk for your practice—at least at first.

The problem is that these relationships don't tend to last long. While adding associates in the same modality seems like a great way to take your practice to the next level, one of two things tends to happen: either the associate becomes frustrated because he's not growing fast enough and leaves your practice, or the associate learns, grows, comes into his own, and decides that he wants to have something of his own, too. When associates leave for either reason, they tend to become your competition in the process.

The associate arrangement is low-risk, up front, and simple. The disadvantages are that it has a shorter life span and can create competition.

Rent a room (lease)

Also quite common is the simpler approach of renting space in your current practice to another practitioner.

The benefit of this approach is that it's extremely easy to do. It only takes a simple agreement and you've got someone contributing to your monthly expenses. The drawback is that this arrangement almost always creates two separate practices in the same space. The person renting space from you is likely to be building *her own* practice, not yours. Regardless of their profession, whether they're duplicators or diversifiers, renters own their own clientele.

When you rent space in your clinic to someone, you are indeed transforming from a practice into a business. The difference is that you're now in the *real estate* business, not the health care one. The person renting space from you isn't helping much with your clients—you're simply her landlord, and the growth of that business is limited solely to how much rent she pays.

When you share space with people, over time those professionals will come to be associated with *you*. Even though they may be simply paying you rent, if they're working in your space then they automatically become part of the image of your business.

The advantages of rental arrangements are that they're simple, immediate, and they provide predictable cash flow. The disadvantages are that you're limiting your earnings and opening yourself up to potential reputation issues.

Employee (salary/wage)

Hiring other CAM professionals—in essence, giving them regular-paying jobs—is far less common. But, like any other relationship, it offers its own advantages.

When you hire an employee, you're hiring a person to work for your business, period. That person works with the clients of *your business*, not her own. She doesn't build her own practice.

She may have her own roster of clients, but those clients belong to *your* business. If the employee decides to leave, she leaves everything and starts from scratch elsewhere.

The downside, of course, is the risk of being obligated to pay a salary to someone. If you hire someone, you may need to pay her even if she doesn't see clients. If your practice is relatively new, paying a salary to another practitioner can become a very expensive proposition.

The advantages of hiring are that you own everything and you secure high earning potential in the long run. The disadvantages are that it's a more complex arrangement with higher financial risk at up front.

Contract (per hour/per day)

Your relationship with your new practitioner can also be at the other end of the spectrum from the long-term commitment of full-time employment. Perhaps you only need someone infrequently to start with. An example might be a massage therapist who offers services at corporate events. Periodically, this therapist needs to bring five or six other therapists to an event or a business site to provide massage services. However, it may not be frequent enough to hire them full time or justify having an associate agreement. For this type of arrangement, simple contract work is all that's needed.

The customers (in this case, the corporation running the event) still "belong" to the massage business owner. The other therapists are simply paid for short-term services. It's a simple, low-risk way to get help. You don't get the stability you might from having the same people around all the time, but your obligation as the business owner is minimal.

The advantages of having contract workers are that the arrangement is low-risk and easy with no obligations on your part. The disadvantages are reduced loyalty and the possibility of paying more expensive hourly or daily rates.

There are hybrid arrangements of these four approaches, and many other variations. You could hire an associate who sees *your* clients, for example, not her own, and who is paid as an independent contractor per day or on a fee split. You could rent space to someone who also helps with your clients. You might start a new person on a contract basis, then transition to an employee relationship. There is a myriad of arrangements happening in practices all around you.

Deciding which relationship is right for you depends on many factors, including your goals, your risk tolerance, and the size of your client base. To help decide, ask yourself the following questions:

- How busy is your practice? How quickly can a new practitioner build a client base in your office?
- How much risk are you willing to assume?
- Who will "own" the clients?
- Do you need your new practitioner to sign a non-competition contract?
- How does everyone make money?
- Does the amount of money this new diversifier or duplicator generates for your practice increase over time? Are there maximums or minimums on a fee split, for example?
- How long do you want this relationship to last?
- Would the new practitioner allow you to take more time away from your business without feeling like your clients are being underserved?
- If this person walked away in a year, what would the impact on your business be? Could she be easily replaced? Would she become competition? Would she be taking something of value with her when she left?
- Are you willing to pay this person even when she doesn't have clients? Or only when she's treating someone?

Leaving the valley, step #3: Make the relationships work

Deciding to add more people to your practice is a huge step for many practitioners. If you've done it, or if you're on your way, we salute you. You're not only doing something great for yourself, but you're also creating opportunity for other practitioners at the same time.

Making the relationship work, however, requires another set of skills. Below are the ones that we've found make the biggest difference in successfully adding other people to the mix.

Choose carefully

While you may find it easy to know exactly which *professional* you need, it can be harder to find the right *person*. After years of recruiting, hiring, firing, and hiring again, we've found a simple three-step system that helps us find people who are a great fit:

1. Find candidates by networking

We rarely advertise unless the position requires a very specific or rare credential. We network with clients, our staff, and other professionals in the community who know us. We ask them if they know of anyone they could recommend who would be a fit for our business. It saves us the time and expense of advertising and wading through hundreds of resumes and letters, guessing at who might be a fit and who might not be.

2. Trust first impressions

Our first interviews are very short and often by phone only. We have a brief, casual conversation to answer any questions that candidates might have. Since we're hiring first and foremost for fit and personality, that call is usually enough to weed out the people who aren't suitable. If we don't get a good feeling, then we don't go any further. If you know that you're not a good judge of people, have someone else help you with this step.

3. Test-drive everyone

Once we've narrowed down the field, we test-drive the people we're considering hiring. We pay them for a half to a full day of time and watch how they fit and how they work. At the end of the day, we get the input of our whole team to help make our decision. It's well worth the small financial investment to avoid a costly mistake that could span months or years.

Is this a foolproof system? No. Occasionally you'll get a false negative—someone you misjudge on the phone, for example, who might have been a great candidate. But those false negatives are a small price to pay for the high percentage of exceptional people you'll find to join your team with the least amount of effort.

Build systems

One of the biggest concerns that practitioners have when adding more people to the mix is that different people do things differently. What if they don't do things the way you do? What if they don't pull their weight?

The first solution is to make sure you've hired the right people for the right reasons. That'll go a long way toward addressing this issue. But if you need things done a certain way, and if you don't want new people to make *more* work for you instead of less, then you need systems.

"Systems" are repeatable steps for doing the same tasks over and over. They're like recipes for getting work done, or formulas for a specific result.

It's not hard to create recipes for your practice. It does, however, take some self-observation and introspection. If you're hiring a duplicator, you'll need to observe how *you* work with clients and capture the critical parts of that on paper so that someone else can do it. If you're hiring a diversifier, you'll need to be even more observant (or consider getting help from someone who understands the other profession better than you do).

Systems are about deciding what's *important*. You can't always control every detail in a service business, but you can control the things that define your difference and deliver the care that you've become known for and proud of.

Coach, train, and mentor

Systems only work if people use them. And they only use them if someone *teaches* them how to use them first. That's especially important in health care, where mistakes can have far-reaching consequences.

Unless the people you add to your business are completely separate from you and simply renting space, you'll need to make a commitment to your new role as teacher. It requires an investment of time up front, but it's critical to your long-term success. And you'll need to be strict in your commitment, scheduling time for that purpose alone. Don't wing it—take the time to do the job completely.

Get serious about your finances

If you've ever worked as an associate, you know how straightforward your bookkeeping can be. The revenue comes in, you give a percentage (or a flat amount) to the clinic, and other than a few expenses like advertising, insurance, and continuing education, the rest goes in your pocket. When your practice is made up of only you, it's not hard to have a rough idea of how profitable you are. Selling your own time has very few "hard" costs. There are no ingredients, materials, supplies, or fuel. When you start selling *other* people's time, though, you need to be more careful. Things that put a decent amount of money in your pocket when *you* were doing them may put you out of business when someone else does them unless you keep an eye on profitability.

When you start transitioning from a practice to a business, figuring out how much money is *yours* can be harder to estimate. If a client spends $200 at your office but you've got five staff members, a larger clinic, and dozens (or even hundreds) of different creditors, how much of that $200 is yours?

When you're choosing new products, paying staff, or buying new treatment tools, you'll need to know how *profitable* you are. Sure, you might be able to charge a hefty fee for your new health assessment tool, but if it takes three hours and two staff members to operate it, is the fee hefty enough?

To find success in business you'll need solid information on your finances. Understanding your financial health helps you set prices, make better business decisions, and have a true picture of your business at all times. Ensuring that your business creates profit makes it worth more, which in turn gives you more options in the future.

If you don't do it already, now is the time to get regular, accurate financial reports from someone who knows what they're doing. That might be you or you may need to add people to your team (like a bookkeeper and accountant, for example). Getting your financial house in order is critical to making your way out of the valley.

Protect yourself where necessary

Things don't always work out. When you add new people to your business, you also add new personalities, needs, wants and visions. Choosing people carefully will go a *long* way in making things easier, but it's wise to get the small details in order, too. Do you need non-compete or non-solicit agreements to protect the client base you've carefully built? Have you carefully spelled out the responsibilities of your and the others in your business so that you can refer back to those details in the event of future disputes?

There are many ways to protect yourself and your assets. Most are fairly straightforward, and getting a little advice isn't usually that costly.

Leaving the valley, step #4: Create business time

As a practitioner you were taught to do one thing well: practice the art of health care.

To do it, you were trained in the application of a specific set of tools, strategies, and philosophies. Over time it became your job to assess, poke, question, prod, needle, adjust, prescribe, discuss, support, comfort, manipulate, rub, and do a multitude of other health care-related tasks.

Those tasks became the activities around which you schedule your time. Your day is arranged by what you do at what time, to which client.

Shifting from practice to business not only requires that you learn a new set of skills (such as managing and leading others), but it also requires that you have *time* to do those things.

You can't successfully transition from practice to business unless you create time specifically for working "on" your business as opposed to working "in" it. You need time to do the things that make your business work—to grow your client base, to create and maintain systems, to track your success, to train, lead, and manage others, and eventually to consider going a step further by training *others* to train, lead, and manage.

That time can only come from one of two places: as extra time carved out of your personal life, or as time carved out of your existing time in practice.

Right now, it's likely that in your practice, the person who provides the treatments is *you*. You're the one who runs the machines, inserts the needles, prescribes the remedies, and examines the client. You do the stuff that directly makes the money. One of the easiest ways to create time to work *on* your business is to do *less* of that.

What does this mean in very simple terms? It means that if you're chiropractor, you're going to have to let another DC begin to treat clients. If you're an acupuncturist, you'll have to let someone else do some of the needling. If you're a nutritionist, it's time to let someone else work through those diet plans and diaries. If you want to reach as many people as possible and still maintain a life outside your office, then you're going to have to give up some of your work as the healer and take on more work as the healing business *owner*. In short, it's time to get a new job.

What does that new job look like? It looks, for the most part, like continuing to work the principles of this book: growing yourself, growing your business, and finding a healthy balance in your life. It looks like many of the things you've been doing along the way, but the difference is that you're going to give more time to those things and less to the actual job of being a health professional.

Should you stop providing care altogether? In many traditional businesses, yes. To grow past a certain point, the owner needs to stop packaging, answering the phones, fixing the computers, and buying supplies, not to mention delivering the actual product or service that the company provides. But health care is special. If helping people really makes you tick, you may want to keep your hand in it. At least for now. For most practitioners, making this shift is about doing *less*, as opposed to doing *none*. It's not about leaving the valley and never looking back. It's about having the choice of entering the valley when you choose to.

The choice, of course, is yours. Just remember that life in the valley is a game of balance, and you should be very careful how you choose to find the time to work on your business.

Other ways to leave the valley

Making the decision to become a CAM practitioner and completing your education are heady times. You're filled with energy and vision. For most of us, it's a time when we think only of how we can help others and how we will do it for the rest of our lives. We can't wait to get started.

The Practitioner's Journey offers you a way to keep that energy and enthusiasm, or to regain your passion if you've lost it. But we also need to do something else: we need to recognize that things change. Much will happen in our lifetimes, and much of that will be unpredictable. Will you still want to be a healer in a decade? We hope so, but we respect the fact that you may not. And so should you. You should also accept that life throws out curve balls once in a while.

What will you do if you no longer want to practice? What will you do if you're no longer *able* to practice? What if you change careers? What if you find a new passion or a new opportunity? What if an illness or accident means you can't practice any longer? What if you fall in love with someone 5,000 miles away?

In those moments, your greatest opportunity will be to have *choice*. To be able to choose a new career—or a new life—and to have the years of work you put into your practice offer you one final gift: *to be able to sell what you've built.*

The challenge, of course, is that it's difficult to sell what you don't own. And in the world of business, ownership is not always as obvious as it seems.

Consider Amanda. She's got a busy practice running with seven other practitioners. Each one is an associate with his or her own clients and works on a fee split. It's easy, it's low risk, and it's delivering a decent amount of cash each month. What happens, though, if Amanda decides to sell her practice? A smart buyer will realize that those seven practitioners could leave at any time and take their clients with them. A smart buyer will realize that the associate income has *some* value, of course, but not as much value as it would have if all the associates were *employees* of the clinic, seeing the *clinic's* clients as opposed to their own. The acupuncturist might leave, for example, but the client belongs to the clinic and can be seen by the acupuncturist who replaces the outgoing one.

The message here is clear: if you're going to make the effort to transition to creating a business instead of a practice, you should also make the effort to ensure that the business you build has *value*.

You can create equity in your business in many ways. Here are three that stand out:

1. Clients

Who owns the client? The answer, of course, is that none of us "own" our clients. But who owns their files and contact information? Who's earned their loyalty and permission to contact them? In other words, *who owns their attributes as customers of the business?* Can the people that work with you take their files with them? If they leave to start their own practice, do their clients go with them?

Many practitioners don't realize just how much value their client "database" is worth. Other than the physical assets of a practice like the equipment and furniture, the bulk of its value is in the loyalty of customers and the ability and permission to contact them.

2. Real estate

Real estate is a way for practitioners to build something of value by doing what many need to do anyway: pay for space to offer their services. Over the course of 20 years of practice, you can pay someone hundreds of thousands of dollars in rent or more, and have nothing to show for it. Or, you could own your own million-dollar building.

By taking on a small amount of risk and a little extra effort, a long career in practice can be topped off by owning a valuable piece of real estate.

3. Intellectual property

Do you have unique health care protocols? Your own special supplements? Patents? They all have value and represent something you own and you can sell if you choose to.

The identity of your business, or its "brand" also has value. Your brand is a business "personality" that can be represented by the name, symbols, slogans, logos, fonts, etc. used by your business. A strong brand has value in the form of goodwill, trademarks, and more, and can be sold just like real estate and customers.

Remember your difference that we defined earlier? If that difference is associated with a brand then that brand carries some of that difference and has value. What's your brand? Imagine you're trying to sell your business. Are you selling your name (for example, "Bob Smith, DC") or a business that *anyone* can operate, like "The Spinal Spa"?

THE DECISION OF THE VALLEY: TO STAY OR GO

If you're any good at this health care stuff—and you probably are—you're going to eventually become *busy*. Our current unhealthy culture and struggling conventional care system are only going to increase the flow of clients to your practice. Unless you burn bridges and turn your lines in the sand into walls and barricades, clients will still arrive in the valley of your practice.

It's tempting, though, to think that you can do just that—
build such clear lines between practice and life that you can stay
in the valley, toeing the line, striking the balance. But life in the
valley has a way of sneaking up on you. We've all seen it. After a
few years, the busy acupuncturist realizes that she's ...well, *really*
busy. She sees clients all day, sometimes on weekends. The
chiropractor stays late to do the bookkeeping and pay the bills.
The naturopath gets emergency calls at home.

They'd all like to take more time off, but it costs thousands
of dollars in lost client revenue to do it. And although they're
billing a decent amount, a realization is slowly seeping into their
consciousness: they don't own a business, they own a *job*.

When that realization occurs to you, there's a solid chance
that you're going to sleep less, love less, laugh less, and live less.
You're going to wake up and know what it really means to have
arrived in Burnout. The valley that seemed like Shangri-La can
quickly become a nightmare landscape. And what if you *can*
manage all those clients? For the practitioners who thrive on this
and can effectively juggle the demands of solo practice, there's
still a limit to how many people they can help.

But don't forget the little detail of that signpost in the rubble. The one revealing that perhaps Success is a little farther
ahead. The clue that tells us the journey isn't over. That makes us
wonder *is this all there is?* It's the stuff midlife crises are made of.

For those practitioners, life in the valley isn't enough. It's
not enough to work with clients in every available moment and
still have to turn away some in need. It's not enough to limit their
income based on the limits of their time. And for many, it's not
enough to be locked in place, unable to discover what comes next
in the journey.

But it can work for some.

The greatest challenge of the valley isn't about finding balance or a way to help when you're out of time. **The greatest
challenge of life in the valley is to decide if it's enough.** That
signpost in the rubble was pointing to Success, but which direction is Success? Is it ahead, or are you already there?

In the end, that's your decision to make.

Acupuncturist, author, and business coach Kevin Doherty had this to say about trying to make solo practice work:

> "*I think it is possible to make a solid six-figure income as a solo practitioner and have a life outside of the practice, but the truth is that this is unfortunately pretty rare. You have to be pretty developed both personally and professionally to handle a high client volume and set healthy boundaries so you don't take it home with you or just end up pretty much living at your office.*"[10]

That's the reality: finding financial success and work-life balance in solo practice is a tough job. But it can be done. Kevin earned a six-figure income in solo practice working less than four days a week—but he might be the exception.

Many practitioners do find joy simply in practice. They're content with an income based on selling time, and they're comfortable with the reality that their income has limited ways in which it can grow beyond a certain point. They can reconcile the idea of simply saying "no" to clients when they get too busy. For those practitioners—the ones who can draw clear lines in the sand and are content with remaining in practice, not business—Success really *is* in the valley. For them, the sign points to where they *are*, not further ahead.

The question is whether or not that's *you*.

If, like in our story, you find yourself wondering what's ahead, then staying in the valley may not be for you. If you're frustrated by an inability to reach more people, or if you have difficulty saying "no" and staying in balance, maybe it's time to consider exploring a little farther afield. If you want to earn more, but not necessarily work more, then you'll need to leave the valley. For you, the signpost for Success is pointing onward, out of the comfort of the steady and familiar canyon walls and over the rocks to what lies beyond. For you, practice won't do. It may do for a while, but likely not forever.

The great thing is that you don't need to decide to leave the valley now. If you've made it this far, you can enjoy the fruits of your labor for as long as like. But when you find your mind wandering to the sign in the rubble, asking, *Is this all there is?* you'll know it's time to make a change.

If you're trying to decide, remember this: not everyone should run a business. But you shouldn't *not* run one because you're afraid that you don't have what it takes, or because you feel it's somehow inconsistent with a life as a healer.

Insights From the Valley

The valley is a deceiving place in practice that almost all practitioners arrive at when they've attracted enough clients. On the surface it seems attractive, but it has the potential to lead us to burnout.

There are two ways to deal with the valley:

LINES IN THE SAND

Draw careful lines boundaries around your time, money and health as a practitioner.

THE LONG LEVER

Leave the valley by transforming your practice into a true business with multiple practitioners.

EPILOGUE
The Summit

"If the path be beautiful, let us not ask where it leads."

-Anatole France

*T*he sun is setting in the valley behind you as you pull yourself over the last rock. You've reached the summit of the cliff wall.

You turn and catch your breath in awe.

A majestic landscape stretches out before you. In the distance, you can see the winding river and the path that follows it— the very same path that brought you here. It fades away in the distance, curving from the entrance to the valley in a great arc to the north.

You've come a long way and you're filled with the glow of accomplishment. You look out again over the path, remembering the challenges along the way. The dark cave that marked what was missing in you and your practice. The cold river that separated you from the people you could help. The boulder that prevented you from moving closer to Success. And finally the valley, that strange place of elation and despair that you've just come from. It lies below you, and you watch spellbound from your new vantage point as the waterfall pours from the canyon walls, tumbling into mist hundreds of feet below and billowing out over the vibrant canopy of the forest.

It's been quite a journey. You feel an extraordinary sense of peace as you watch the sun dip below the horizon and the stars slowly emerge overhead.

The months that follow are busy ones. Since making your way to the summit above the valley the first time, you find you can now do it with ease. You still spend much of your time in the valley, helping others and also helping the helpers who you've invited to join you.

But your time in the valley seems somehow different now. One day, as you sit on the summit and gaze at the panorama before you, you realize what it is: your time in the valley feels different now because you're *choosing it.* Leaving the valley was a challenge, but it's given you back a flexibility you that you'd lost somewhere along your journey.

And in that moment, you realize what Success is: *it's the freedom to choose.*

In the coming weeks you put your newfound freedom to use. It isn't long before you begin to explore the summit further and discover that, contrary to what you had originally thought, the path doesn't end there. In fact, the path splinters into many new ones that head off in a myriad of directions, each with its own twists and turns, its own terrain, and its own challenges.

You find yourself spending more of your free time outside the valley, exploring new paths and new options, but always returning to the summit for the panorama view of your journey so far. Often, you venture into the valley with a new skip in your step to do what you've always wanted to do: *help.*

One day, you follow a path farther than you ever have before, passing through a thick wood and emerging in a wide clearing at the edge of another forest. From here, the path winds its way into the woods again, disappearing from sight.

And at the edge of the path is a signpost.

You look. Blink. And look again.

It's the signpost. The one marking path into the forest that you saw when you first began your journey so long ago.

Reaching into your pocket, you pull out a weathered scrap of paper. It's worn and yellowed, but still quite legible:

Fellow Practitioner,

Welcome to the journey. The good news is that Success is not as far away as you may have been led to believe. To reach it, you need only what you carry with you right now. The rest you will find along the path.

The rules are few and simple. To reach Success you need only do two things: follow the path to its end, and help as many people along the way as you can.

Good luck and safe passage.

You smile in recollection. It's been quite a journey.

As you turn to go, you hear the sound of cheerful whistling carried to you on the wind. You turn toward it, and far in the distance you see a figure walking toward the path where you stand.

You look down fondly at the note in your hand. With one last look around, you tack the parchment back onto the signpost where you first found it so long ago, smile, and walk back into the forest.

The End

AFTERWORD
Love, life and legacy in health care

"You're remarkable. How dare you waste it."

-Seth Godin, *The Dip*

t the heart of this book is the idea that you can help more people, find financial success, and maintain a healthy work-life balance all at the same time. But how can that be? How can you do less and get more?

Part of the answer lies in the definition of "doing less." The truth is, *The Practitioner's Journey* doesn't ask you to do less; it asks you to do *better*. To move beyond the simple premise of selling time for money and take you and your practice to a new level where what you offer is more than just your time. When you add more to your time—your ability to think and strategize and your ability to assume some risk, for example—you become something more than just a health care practitioner. You become a provider of *value*, someone who infuses all aspects of your practice with intelligence, passion, and wisdom. You become someone who, in return, is rewarded.

And what is that reward? Without question, part of that reward is financial. Following the principles of *The Practitioner's Journey* will help you find greater income and build something of value that is yours to sell. But there are more variables to the equation than simply money. The "profits" of *The Practitioner's Journey* extend to other areas of your life, and to the lives of others, too. There's more to successful business than meets the eye. Don't abandon the idea of a world where commerce and health care can find a synergy that serves everyone.

As CAM practitioners, we've known for years that there is more to health than conventional medicine. We stand now at a turning point in health care that will broaden the minds and expand the health of more people than ever before. To turn that corner, however, requires more than skilled healers. It requires professional success.

Keep growing. That's what allows you to give back. To hire a new grad in your field. To grow your profession and its standing in the world health community. To coach and nurture a new practitioner into becoming a better one. To tack your note to the start of the path and encourage another practitioner to make her own journey.

If you want to help more clients, reach more people, and heal more lives, then do this: *find your way to Success.* If you want to change the world, then start with yourself. Strive for excellence as a practitioner *and* a business owner. Be a mentor, a role model, and a leader by example.

Be a beacon for the ones to come.

Thanks for reading. Good luck with your practice and your business.

Dan Clements & Tara Gignac, ND
May 2010

RECOMMENDED READING

Book Yourself Solid: The Fastest, Easiest and Most Reliable System for Getting More Clients Than You Can Handle Even if You Hate Marketing and Selling, Michael Port, John Wiley & Sons, Inc., 2006

The Go-Giver: A Little Story About a Powerful Business Idea, Bob Burg and John David Mann, Portfolio, 2007

Go-Giver's Sell More, Bob Burg and John David Mann, Portfolio, 2010

The Diamond Cutter: The Buddha on Strategies for Managing Your Business and Your Life, Geshe Michael Roach, Doubleday, 2000

Rich Dad, Poor Dad, Robert T. Kiyosaki and Sharon L. Lechter, Business Plus, 2000

The E-Myth Revisited: Why Most Small Businesses Don't Work and What to Do About It, Michael E. Gerber, Harper Collins, 1995

Blue Ocean Strategy: How to Create Uncontested Market Space and Make the Competition Irrelevant, W. Chan Kim, Renee Mauborgne, Harvard Business School Press, 2005

Made to Stick: Why Some Ideas Survive and Others Die, Chip Heath and Dan Heath, Random House, 2007

Creating Customer Evangelists: How Loyal Customers Become a Volunteer Sales Force Ben McConnell, Jackie Huba, Guy Kawasaki, Kaplan Business, 2007

ENDNOTES

[1] http://www.stevepavlina.com/blog/2005/02/the-best-place-to-invest-your-money/

[2] http://sethgodin.typepad.com/seths_blog/2009/12/the-first-transaction.html

[3] Via John Weeks of The Integrator Blog, who heard it at a conference sponsored by the Health Forum/American Hospital Association in Honolulu, Hawaii, February 1999.

[4] For an excellent look at the business model that drives WCA, see Issue No. 16 (November 2006) of *The Integrator Blog*, available online at http://www.theintegratorblog.com

[5] September 2006 issue of *Acupuncture Today*

[6] To learn more about community acupuncture, consider Lisa Rohleder's books, *The Remedy, Integrating Acupuncture into American Healthcare* and *Acupuncture Is Like Noodles: The Little Red (Cook) Book of Working Class Acupuncture* available at communityacupuncturenetwork.org

[7] Obesity Facts. Feb, 2009. Paul-Ebhohimhen V, Avenell A. A systematic review of the effectiveness of group versus individual treatments for adult obesity.

[8] http://www.word-detective.com/back-e2.html, *In Love With Norma Loquendi* by William Safire

[9] Skip Van Meter, "The Long-Term Futility of a Solo Practitioner," Community Acupuncture Network forum blog, July 16, 2007 http://www.communityacupuncturenetwork.org/forum/read.php?32,3965

[10] From an interview we did with Kevin in October, 2009. Read the whole thing at http://alternativehealthpractice.com/2009/10/a-six-figure-income-in-3-5-days-per-week-practice-wisdom-from-kevin-doherty.html

SPREADING THE WORD
How to Help Your Fellow Practitioners

We all know that CAM works.

That is, you know it and we know it. But the public doesn't always know.

We believe that the single biggest way to help CAM thrive in our culture is to help its practitioners thrive in *business*. That's why we wrote this book, and it's why we'd like to ask for your help.

If you've enjoyed this book, please tell a fellow practitioner. Better yet, give her a copy. You can buy her one, but don't be afraid to give her the one you're reading right now—sharing is just fine with us. That's how good ideas are spread.

Here are some more ideas to help you tack *your* note to our figurative signpost:

- Write a review of *The Practitioner's Journey* on Amazon.com or your favorite online bookstore.
- Recommend it to your professor, instructor, dean, or someone in your school bookstore. Suggest that they add this book to the bookstore shelves and include it in school curriculums.
- Recommend this book to your professional association.
- Invite us to speak at your next conference or professional convention.
- Email, blog, tweet, favorite, or otherwise share it socially

Thanks for helping us reach more practitioners!

Safe travels,

-D & T

ABOUT THE AUTHORS

DAN CLEMENTS & TARA GIGNAC, ND own and operate Stone-Tree Clinic in Collingwood, Ontario.

Their practice management writing has appeared in numerous publications, and their popular practice growth blog is read by thousands of practitioners from a diverse range of health care professions.

Their previous book, *Escape 101: Sabbaticals Made Simple*, has appeared in *The Wall Street Journal*, *Forbes*, *Success Magazine*, and on numerous A-list blogs.

You can reach them at www.practitionersjourney.com.

CPSIA information can be obtained at www.ICGtesting.com
Printed in the USA
LVOW121940060212

267343LV00005B/17/P